Economic Decline

Economic Decline

Unraveling the United States' Downturn

ALINA HAZEL

UNIEK ENTERPRISES

CONTENTS

Chapter 7: Potential Solutions

7.1 Policy recommendations for economic revitalization

7.2 The role of public-private partnerships in recovery efforts

Chapter 8: Future Outlook

8.1 Projections for the trajectory of the U.S. economy

8.2 Key factors that could influence economic recovery

Chapter 9: Conclusion

9.1 Recapitulation of major findings

9.2 Call to action for stakeholders in addressing economic decline

INTRODUCTION

In recent years, the economic environment of the United States, which is a worldwide economic superpower, has been subjected to a great amount of examination and analysis. Through an examination of historical precedents, current indications, and future prospects, the book "Economic Decline: Unraveling the United States' Downturn" digs into the complexity and nuances of the nation's economic issues. In order to provide readers with a more nuanced knowledge of the causes that are at play, this in-depth investigation tries to dissect the complex nature of the economic crisis.

Contextualization of the Past:

It is essential to first research the historical context of economic fluctuations in the United States in order to acquire an understanding of the current economic issues that are being faced. In order to get useful insights into the cyclical patterns that have characterized the nation's financial history, it is worth examining the pivotal occasions that have occurred throughout the nation's economic evolution. The story lays the groundwork for comprehending the repetitive nature of economic issues by establishing a foundation by drawing analogies to previous episodes of economic decline.

Indicators of the Current Economic Situation:

The examination of the modern economic indicators that shed light on the issues that are currently being faced is the central focus of the investigation. Trends in the Gross Domestic Product (GDP), rates of unemployment, and inflationary pressures are all subjected to careful analysis. This part serves as a diagnostic instrument, illuminating the clinical indications of the economic collapse that has been occurring. Conducting a comprehensive examination of these indicators serves as the foundation for comprehending the magnitude and the effects of the economic slump.

Factors Affecting the Global Economy:

There is a significant connection between the interdependence of the current global economy and the economic issues that the United States is facing. The economic trajectory of the nation is substantially influenced by the dynamics of international trade as well as developments in the global economy throughout the world. This section sheds light on the ways in which external forces influence and are influenced by the economic downturn by examining the intricate relationships that exist between the economy of the United States of America and the larger global context within which it operates.

The Implications for Politics and Public Policy:

It is the actions and policy frameworks of the government that play a significant impact in determining the outcomes of the economy. The impact of governance on the economic trajectory of the nation is investigated through the assessment of political and policy implications. The story illustrates the delicate dance between political choices and economic realities by examining existing policies and their success. This provides readers with insights into the complexities of economic governance. Through this evaluation, the narrative highlights the intricate dance.

Consequences on Society:

In addition to the numerical measurements, the deterioration of the economy has significant repercussions for society. There are a number of aspects that contribute to the impact of the economic crisis, including social and cultural implications, income inequality, and a widening wealth gap. Through the use of this part, readers are encouraged to contemplate the human element of economic issues, which helps to cultivate empathy and comprehension for individuals who are impacted by the economic slump.

Obstacles that are Unique to the Industry:

Various sectors of the economy are affected by the economic downturn in a variety of different ways. This part of the article takes a detailed look at the difficulties that industries including manufacturing, technology, and services are currently facing. Through an examination of the particulars that are specific to the industry, readers are able to obtain an understanding of the ripple effects that have an impact on innovation, technological advancement, and the general economic resiliency of the nation.

Concerning the Possible Solutions:

To combat the deterioration of the economy, a proactive approach that incorporates workable answers is required. In this section, a full investigation of prospective solutions is presented, together with policy recommendations for the revitalization of the economy. The investigation of public-private partnerships helps to highlight the importance of working together in order to successfully navigate the complicated path that leads to recovery.

The outlook for the future:

The story comes to a close with a perspective that looks into the future, predicting the path that the economy of the United States would take and describing the most important things that could have an impact on the economic recovery. The future outlook section offers readers with a road map for understanding the potential pathways toward a more robust economic future. This is accomplished by analyzing trends, upcoming technologies, and global dynamics.

A comprehensive investigation that navigates the historical, current, and future facets of the nation's economic issues, "Economic Decline: Unraveling the United States' Downturn" is a book that discusses the economic decline of the United States. The narrative reveals the complex web of reasons that have contributed to the economic crisis by deconstructing economic data, investigating global effects, analyzing political ramifications, and taking into consideration the consequences for society.

The study is given more depth by the investigation of industry-specific difficulties, potential solutions, and real-world case studies. This provides readers with a comprehensive grasp of the economic landscape. The prospective viewpoint emphasizes the dynamic character of economic trajectories and places an emphasis on the significance of flexibility and collaboration in the process of charting a course toward a future that is more robust.

This all-encompassing investigation encourages readers to engage critically with the complexity that is at play in order to solve the mystery of the economic downturn that has been occurring in the United States. The narrative contributes to ongoing discussions about economic regeneration, policy innovation, and the imperative for resilience in the face of economic crises by promoting an informed and nuanced perspective. Other topics that are discussed include the necessity of resilience.

1. **Brief overview of the economic landscape**

    The landscape of the economy is a large and ever-changing terrain that is formed by a myriad of elements that have an impact on the prosperity and well-being of nations, organizations, and individuals. The understanding of the economic landscape is vital for policymakers, businesses, and the general public because it provides insights into the conditions that are currently in place, the difficulties that are being faced, and the opportunities that are being presented through economic activities. In order to provide light on the fundamental principles that support the functioning of economies, the purpose of this overview is to travel through the essential elements of the economic landscape.

    The fundamentals of the current economic landscape:

    The economic landscape is formed upon the fundamental principles of supply and demand, where the interactions between buyers and sellers influence the allocation of resources. This is the foundation upon which the economic landscape is built. As the core of economic analysis, this fundamental concept, which is frequently summarized by the principles of supply and demand, serves as the foundation. Through the interaction of these forces, pricing, output, and consumption are all influenced, which ultimately results in the establishment of a dynamic equilibrium within the economic system.

    Indicators of the Macroeconomic Process:

    The monitoring of major macroeconomic indicators, which offer a snapshot of the state of an economy as a whole, is an essential component in gaining an understanding of the economic environment. There are a number of fundamental measures that economists and policymakers pay special attention to, including the Gross Domestic Product (GDP), unemployment rates, inflation, and interest rates. Specifically, gross domestic product (GDP) serves as an all-encompassing measurement of the total economic output of a country, while also representing the size of the economy and its growth trajectory.

The Structures of the Market and the Competition:

The landscape of the economy is varied, consisting of a variety of market systems that influence the actions of both consumers and corporations. Every market structure, from those that are totally competitive to those that are monopolies, has an impact on market price, production, and innovation. A market's efficiency and the manner in which economic advantages are distributed are frequently determined by the level of competition that exists within that market. It is necessary for policymakers to find a middle ground between encouraging competition and regulating industries in order to guarantee equitable practices.

Globalization and the Trade of International Goods:

Within the context of an era marked by growing interconnection, the economic landscape stretches beyond the borders of individual nations. Globalization and international trade are two factors that significantly contribute to the formation of economic dynamics. On a global scale, nations engage in the exchange of commodities, services, and capital, which has the effect of altering comparative advantages, specialization, and the distribution of wealth. Because of this, the economic landscape is a complicated tapestry that is weaved together by the threads of international trade agreements and various trade agreements.

Labor Markets and Human Capital:

The labor market has a significant impact on the economic landscape. Wages, employment rates, and the general productivity of an economy are all determined by the quantity of labor that is available and the amount of workers that is in demand. One of the most important factors that contributes to economic expansion is human capital, which refers to the competencies, expertise, and capabilities of the labor force. The quality of human capital and, as a result, the economic landscape are both influenced by policies that invest in education, training, and workforce development of their respective populations.

Policies Regarding Monetary and Fiscal Matters:

The policies that governments implement in terms of monetary and fiscal policy are the primary means by which they shape the economic landscape. Monetary policies are implemented by central banks in order to control the amount of money in circulation, interest rates, and inflation. The decisions that are made about budgetary matters, taxing, and expenditure by the government are examples of fiscal policies. The coordination of these policies is intended to achieve the goals of stabilizing the economy, fostering growth, and reducing the damaging effects of economic downturns.

Innovations and technological advancements:
As a result of technical breakthroughs and innovations, the economic environment is continuously undergoing transformation. Existing industries are being reshaped, conventional business models are being disrupted, and new opportunities are being created as a result of the introduction of new technologies such as artificial intelligence, blockchain, and renewable energy. Productivity, efficiency, and general competitiveness of economies are all improved as a result of innovation, which is a driving force behind economic growth.

Considerations Regarding the Environment and The Community:
Over the course of the past few years, environmental and social concerns have become increasingly integrated into the economic landscape. Sustainable development, corporate social responsibility, and ethical business practices are becoming increasingly prominent in today's business sector. When one takes into account the fact that resources are limited and the significance of social well-being, it becomes clear that there is a pressing requirement for an approach to economic operations that is both responsible and balanced.

Monetary Systems and Financial Markets:
The financial markets, which include stock exchanges, bond markets, and currency markets, are essential elements that make up the economic landscape. The allocation of capital is made easier by these markets, which also make it possible for firms to raise funds and offer individuals chances to invest their resources. One of the most important factors in ensuring that the economy remains in a state of equilibrium is the stability and effectiveness of monetary systems, which includes the function of central banks and the international monetary framework.

Disparities in the Economy and the Redistribution of Wealth:
One of the defining characteristics of the economic landscape is the manner in which wealth and income are distributed within a society itself. When economic inequality is severe, it can result in social discontent and provide a barrier to the growth of the economy over the long run. Concerning the subject of how to combat inequality through the implementation of policies such as progressive taxation, social safety nets, and inclusive economic policies, policymakers are struggling with several questions.

Ultimately, in order to successfully navigate the economic landscape, one must traverse a terrain that is characterized by complex relationships, dynamic forces, and patterns that are constantly shifting. A number of important factors that contribute to the complexity of the economic landscape have been discussed in this concise summary. These factors include macroeconomic indicators, market structures, globalization, technological improvements, and environmental issues.

Knowledge of the economic environment is not only a matter of academic interest; rather, it is necessary for making well-informed decisions at all levels, including those of the individual, the business, and the government. For the purpose of supporting economic development that is both sustainable and inclusive, it is becoming increasingly important to have a sophisticated understanding of these elements as the global economy continues to undergo change.

2. Significance of understanding economic decline in the United States

The trajectory of the United States economy is an issue of tremendous relevance, with repercussions that extend far beyond the domains of financial markets and the policies of the government. The United States of America, which is a worldwide economic superpower, plays a significantly important part in the process of sculpting the international economic landscape. Therefore, having an understanding of the intricacies of economic decline inside the nation is of multifarious relevance, as it has an impact not only on the well-being of the local population but also on the stability of the global community. Within the scope of this investigation, the fundamental significance of comprehending the economic downturn in the United States is being investigated.

Interconnectedness of the World's Economic System:

In terms of economics, the United States of America is a pivotal player in the international arena. The economic downturn that occurs within its boundaries has repercussions on a worldwide scale, influencing trading partners, investment flows, and the overall stability of the economy around the world. The economic well-being of the United States is inextricably connected with that of other countries thanks to the fact that it is both a consumer of goods and services and a hub for financial operations. As governments, organizations, and individuals all over the world negotiate the interwoven global economic web, it is becoming increasingly important for them to have a comprehensive understanding of the complexities of the economic collapse in the United States.

The Effects on International Markets:

The significance of comprehending the economic downturn that has been occurring in the United States is especially evident when seen in the perspective of international financial markets.

The United States dollar is the principal reserve currency of the globe, and the state of the economy in the United States has a significant impact on the rates of currency exchange, the prices of commodities, and the confidence of investors all over the world. A fall in the economy can cause oscillations in global markets, which can have an impact on investments, trade balances, and the general sentiment of the economy on a regional and worldwide scale.

Supply Chains and International Trade Relations:

Both as a consumer and a producer, the United States of America is a significant actor in the realm of international trade. A fall in the economy can cause disruptions in existing trade links, which can have an effect on the economies of various nations that are export-oriented. Furthermore, the sophisticated worldwide supply chains that are characteristic of modern manufacturing and trade are susceptible to changes in the economic climate in the United States. For nations who are looking to adjust to changes in trade dynamics and supply chain vulnerabilities, it is absolutely necessary to have a full understanding of the economic decline that the United States is experiencing.

Stability of the Global Financial System:

The United States' financial system is an essential component of the global financial system. Because the United States is home to some of the largest banks, financial institutions, and stock exchanges in the world, any disruption in the financial markets of the United States can have repercussions that are felt all over the world. As a result, it is essential for policymakers and financial institutions all over the world to have a solid understanding of the economic downturn that is occurring within the United States. This is because they are formulating strategies to reduce the likelihood of potential systemic risks and to guarantee the stability of the worldwide financial architecture.

The Markets for Energy and Commodities:

Within the realms of energy and commodity markets, the United States of America is a key player. A fall in the economy can shape patterns of energy use, which in turn can have an impact on the global oil and gas markets. As an additional point of interest, the demand for commodities, which can include everything from metals to agricultural items, is strongly connected to the state of the economy in the United States. It is crucial for countries that rely on the export of commodities and the generation of energy to have a comprehensive awareness of the economic collapse that is occurring in the United States.

The Implications for Multinational Corporations of the Following:

There is a worldwide landscape in which multinational corporations (MNCs) operate, and the United States of America frequently serves as a primary market and base for these entities.

It is possible for multinational corporations that have a large exposure to the market in the United States to experience a deterioration in their profitability, expansion ambitions, and overall operations. In order to successfully manage the complexity of a globalized business environment, it is essential for corporate leaders, investors, and legislators to have a solid understanding of the economic climate in the United States.

Relationships between Diplomacy and Geopolitical Conditions:

The strength of a nation's economy is an essential component of the geopolitical influence that it possesses. When evaluating the shifting dynamics of power, it is crucial for diplomats and policymakers around the world to have a solid understanding of the economic downturn that has occurred in the United States. The economic difficulties that are occurring within the United States have the potential to have an impact on diplomatic relations, trade talks, and joint activities pertaining to global issues such as climate change, health crises, and security difficulties.

The Influence on Newly Emerging Markets:

The economic health of major economies such as the United States is constantly monitored by emerging markets, which are frequently more susceptible to the effects of economic shocks from the outside world. It is possible for a decline in the economy of the United States to result in the outflow of money, the depreciation of currency, and economic difficulties in emerging markets. There is a critical need for policy-makers in these countries to have a comprehensive understanding of the economic situation in the United States in order to implement adaptive measures and strengthen their economies against the possibility of spillover effects.

Implications for Society and Culture:

Having a grasp of the economic collapse in the United States has important reper-cussions for both society and culture, in addition to the economic and geopolitical factors that are involved. In many cases, social discontent, political movements, and alterations in the priorities of society are the inevitable outcomes of economic diffi-culties. In order to successfully traverse the intricacies of a society that is undergoing economic upheaval, it is vital for individuals, communities, and governments alike to have a deep grasp of these dynamics.

Iterations of Innovations and Responses to Policy:

In addition to the world of policy development and innovation, the significance of comprehending economic decline extends to the realm of economic decline. For the purpose of formulating effective policy responses, it is vital to have a deep understand-ing of the underlying causes and dynamics of the economic issues that the United States is facing. This information can be utilized by policymakers, economists, and thought leaders in order to design innovative policies with the goals of rejuvenating the economy, encouraging growth that is inclusive, and resolving structural flaws.

The relevance of comprehending the economic downturn in the United States reverberates across a variety of aspects, including those of the global economy, poli-tics, and society. In its role as a pivotal component of the global economy, the United States has a singular position that has a significant impact on the economic well-being and stability of countries all over the world. It is crucial for stakeholders all across the world, including politicians, corporations, individuals, and international organizations, to have a thorough grasp of the economic collapse that is occurring within its boundaries. An understanding that is shared across people helps to create collaboration, resilience, and flexibility in a world where the fortunes of nations are closely connected. This understanding is necessary in order to successfully navigate the obstacles and opportunities given by economic decline.

Chapter 1

Historical Context

In the course of human history, events, ideas, and cultural shifts have been woven together to create a vast and complicated tapestry that is the course of human history. Historical context serves as the backdrop against which narratives are told, and it has the ability to influence the course of events for individuals, societies, and civilizations collectively. In the course of this investigation, we delve into the depths of historical context, tracing its relevance, intricacies, and the significant influence it has on the formation of the world that we live in today.

Establishing the Historical Context By:

When we talk about historical context, we are referring to the conditions, happenings, and cultural atmosphere that surround and have an effect on a specific historical event or time period. It is the more comprehensive framework within which persons and societies function, and it offers the required depth for comprehending the reasons behind actions made in the past, the difficulties they presented, and the results they brought about. By analyzing the historical background, we are able to acquire a better understanding of the factors that influenced the formation of societies, the ideologies that were prevalent at the time, and the dynamics that made key historical moments possible.

The Importance of Being Able to Recognize the Historical Context:

When it comes to interpreting the complexity of the past and generating lessons for the present and the future, having a solid understanding of the historical context is absolutely necessary. It gives us a prism through which we can examine the choices, actions, and repercussions that historical persons and communities made in the past. Furthermore, historical context encourages the development of a nuanced perspective, which challenges too simplified interpretations and acknowledges the varied nature of historical events. By gaining an understanding of the historical context, we are able to acquire an appreciation for the interconnectivity of events, notice patterns, and discover legacies that continue to exist.

The Influence of Social and Cultural Factors:

One of the most important aspects of historical context is the influence that it has had on communities and cultures. Individuals and groups are influenced in their behaviors and attitudes by the cultural norms, values, and belief systems that they adhere to. The study of historical context enables us to gain an understanding of the cultural environment in which individuals lived, thus throwing light on the worldviews, artistic manifestations, religious practices, and social structures that were prevalent during that time period.

No matter if one is investigating the Renaissance in Europe, the Golden Age of Islam, or the Ming Dynasty in China, historical context reveals the intricate web of cultural and social influences that characterized each era.

Structures and Forces of the Economic System:

The conditions and structures of the economy are essential elements that make up the surrounding historical backdrop. There is a significant impact that a society's economic policies, trading routes, and techniques of production have on the growth of that society as well as its connections with the wider globe. For example, the Industrial Revolution was a revolution that brought about a significant change in the structures of the economy. This change resulted in the development of new types of labor, urbanization, and technological developments. Through the examination of historical economic backdrop, one can gain insights into the elements that either facilitated or impeded the growth of the economy, hence influencing the prosperity or difficulties that civilizations have encountered.

Power Structures and the Dynamics of Political Systems:

An unbreakable connection exists between political dynamics and power structures and the historical setting. All of these events, including the rise and fall of empires, the development of political ideologies, and the fights for independence, have their origins deeply ingrained in the historical backdrop of the periods themselves. We are able to get a thorough grasp of the ways in which political dynamics have affected societies throughout the course of history by analyzing political institutions, governance systems, and the interactions that take place between sovereigns and their people. The Enlightenment period, for example, was characterized by a reevaluation of political power and the assertion of individual rights, which had a tremendous influence on the political events that followed.

The progression of technology and the introduction of new ideas:

The historical setting is significantly influenced by the technological breakthroughs that have taken place. Some examples of transformational events that have altered the course of history include the invention of the printing press, the harnessing of steam power, and the birth of the internet. In addition to having an effect on the material conditions of societies, technological breakthroughs also have the ability to transform the cultural, economic, and political landscapes of such nations. We are able to appreciate how breakthroughs have ignited revolutions, triggered societal upheavals, and propelled mankind into new eras of progress when we have a historical understanding of the environment in which scientific advancements have occurred.

Global Interactions and Exchanges:

Beyond the confines of individual nations, historical context encompasses the worldwide interactions and exchanges that have played a significant role in the formation of civilizations.

The Silk Road, the Columbian Exchange, and the Age of Exploration are all examples of times when societies from different regions of the world came into contact with one another and exchanged products, ideas, and technologies with one another. The examination of the historical context of these global contacts offers a comprehensive perspective on the manner in which interconnectivity has been a defining characteristic of human history, exerting an influence on cultures, economics, and outlooks on the world.

Crisis and Conflict:

Both crisis and conflict are inherently present in historical narratives; therefore, it is vital to comprehend the historical context in which these events occurred in order to fully comprehend the intricacies of these occurrences. Whether one is looking at the World Wars, revolutions, or social movements, historical context sheds light on the underlying causes, the contending ideologies, and the geopolitical landscapes that were responsible for setting the stage for these revolutionary periods. By analyzing the historical context of crises, we are able to acquire insights into the circumstances that led to the occurrence of these crises as well as the lessons that these crises can teach us about how to navigate present issues.

Shifts in paradigms and significant cultural revolutions:

The cultural revolutions and paradigm shifts that occur throughout certain periods in history are responsible for the redefining of societies. Existing paradigms were challenged and new ways of thinking evolved during certain epochs, such as the Renaissance in Europe, the Scientific Revolution, and the countercultural movements of the 20th century. These are all examples of epochs. For the purpose of deciphering the intellectual and cultural currents that gave rise to these transformative moments, historical context is essential. This enables us to grasp the significant impact that these events had on molding subsequent eras with which they were associated.

Inheritance and Recollection:

In the context of history, the legacy of historical events and the memory of those events continue to exist as part of the historical context. Historical events have the power to shape the identities and narratives of civilizations, regardless of whether they are recorded through monuments, literature, or collective memory. By gaining an understanding of the ways in which historical events are remembered and celebrated, one can gain insights into the priority and values that are held by a community. In this sense, historical context extends beyond the time boundaries of an event, and it has an impact on the ways in which cultures form their identities and interpret their past.

The historical context serves as the structural foundation upon which our comprehension of the past is constructed.

The factors that have molded societies, the concepts that have inspired human endeavors, and the dynamics that have driven historical events are all brought to light by this. We are able to develop a great awareness for the connectivity of human experiences throughout time and geography when we delve into the rich tapestry of historical context. It is through this exploration that we are able to decode the complexity of the past, learn from the successes and failures of our ancestors, and manage the problems and possibilities that are present in the present and in the future.

1.1 Overview of key economic milestones in U.S. history

A captivating narrative of invention, perseverance, and transformation can be found in the history of the United States' economy. Beginning with its colonial beginnings and culminating in its emergence as a worldwide economic powerhouse, the United States of America has gone through a succession of significant economic milestones that have defined its history and affected the path that would be taken by the economy of the globe. The purpose of this investigation is to present an overview of significant periods in the history of the United States economy. It does so by monitoring the development of economic structures, policies, and technologies that have shaped the economic landscape of the nation.

The Economic Foundations of the Colonial Period (1607-1776):

It is possible to trace the origins of the United States' economy all the way back to its colonial era, which was characterized by the development of agricultural economies, trading networks, and the beginning of several businesses. Cash crops like tobacco and indigo were the primary source of income for the Southern colonies, while the Northern colonies were engaged in activities such as shipbuilding, fishing, and trade. The British Crown utilized mercantilist policies with the intention of exploiting the colonies for the purpose of obtaining raw materials and markets. The economic pressures that resulted from these measures were the catalysts that led to the beginning of the American Revolution.

The beginning of the nation-state (1776–1860):

The creation of the United States of America as an independent nation occurred in the aftermath of the American Revolution for Independence. The recently established country was confronted with a number of economic issues, including the requirement to develop trade links and to establish a stable currency. At the time of its ratification in 1787, the Constitution of the United States of America established a framework for economic governance. This framework gave the federal government the authority to impose taxes and regulate interstate commerce. At the time of the Louisiana Purchase in 1803, the nation's territory was increased, which resulted in the opening of new doors for economic expansion.

The Industrial Revolution and the Market Revolution (1800–1860):

The beginning of the 19th century was marked by a revolutionary period known as the "Market Revolution," which was defined by improvements in transportation (such as the steamboat and the railroad) and communication (the telegraph). The flow of commodities and information was made easier as a result of these innovations, which contributed to the growth of economic interconnection. During this time period, the Industrial Revolution began to take hold, which resulted in the establishment of textile mills, factories, and manufacturing hubs. As a result of this transition from agricultural to industrial economies, the United States experienced a turning point in its economic history. Urbanization and technical innovation became the driving forces behind this transition.

Manifest Destiny and the Westward Expansion of the United States (1803-1890):

In addition to impacting economic pursuits and helping to shape the identity of the nation, the concept of Manifest Destiny was a driving force behind westward expansion. Both migration and commercial activity across the continent were fuelled by events such as the development of the transcontinental railroad, the Oregon Trail, and the California Gold Rush. Not only did the purchase of territory and the opening of the frontier create chances for economic growth, but they also established the groundwork for future economic and demographic expansion.

In the years 1861 to 1877, the Civil War and Reconstruction:

The Civil War was a watershed event in the history of the United States, and it had significant repercussions for the economy. As a result of the struggle, industrialization was accelerated in order to satisfy the requirements of the war, which resulted in greater output and technological innovation. Following the conclusion of the war and throughout the period of Reconstruction, there were efforts made to reconstruct the economy of the South and to incorporate persons who had been formerly enslaved into the labor force. Significant economic and social implications were brought about by the 13th Amendment, which abolished slavery. These repercussions provided the foundation for a new work landscape.

Robber barons in the Gilded Age (1870s-1900): what happened?

The latter half of the 19th century, which is commonly referred to as the Gilded Age, was characterized by rapid industrialization, economic expansion, and the advent of powerful commercial magnates who were known as "Robber Barons." The steel industry, the oil industry, and the financial industry were all dominated by influential figures such as Andrew Carnegie, John D. Rockefeller, and J.P. Morgan. During this time period, there was a consolidation of corporate power, an expansion of railroads, and the formation of labor movements that advocated for the rights of workers.

Reforms undertaken during the Progressive Era (1890-1920):

In response to the significant economic imbalances that existed during the Gilded Age, the Progressive Era came into existence as a means of addressing both social and economic issues. Progressive reforms were implemented with the intention of reducing the influence of monopolies, enhancing working conditions, and addressing concerns regarding social fairness. An effort was made to strike a balance between economic interests and the well-being of society, and the Sherman Antitrust Act of 1890 and the establishment of regulatory entities, such as the Interstate Commerce Commission and the Federal Reserve, were both examples of such efforts.

It was during the Roaring Twenties (1914-1929) that World War I took place

The United States of America experienced substantial economic repercussions as a result of World War I. Following the conclusion of the war, the country became a creditor and went through a period of tremendous economic growth that came to be known as the Roaring Twenties. With the growth of the automotive industry and the expansion of credit, the 1920s witnessed a level of consumption that had never been seen before. In spite of this, the era was also responsible for the Great Depression, which occurred as a result of economic imbalances and excessive speculative activity that contributed to an economic bubble that could not be sustained.

In the years 1929–1941, the Great Depression and the New Deal included:

The crash of the stock market in 1929 was the inciting event that led to the Great Depression, a devastating economic crisis that impacted millions of people in the United States. The unemployment rate skyrocketed, businesses went out of business, and people were put in a precarious financial situation. The New Deal, which consisted of a number of initiatives and changes, was put into effect by President Franklin D. Roosevelt as a response to the economic crisis that was occurring at the time. There was a shift in the role that the government played in the economy as a result of the New Deal, which included measures for social welfare, financial controls, and infrastructural projects.

The Second World War and the Boom That Followed (1941–1996):

In the course of World War II, the United States of America became the "Arsenal of Democracy," supplying the Allied troops with goods and materials. This served as a stimulus for the economic recovery that followed the war. As a result of the war effort, industrial production was boosted, the United States was able to lift itself out of the Great Depression, and it rose to the position of economic leader on a global scale. During the postwar era, the economy experienced remarkable growth, which was driven by the proliferation of the middle class, the development of new technologies, and the suburbanization of neighborhoods.

The struggle for civil rights and the pursuit of economic equality (1950s–1970s):

The Civil Rights Movement was a movement that began in the middle of the 20th century and fought against institutionalized discrimination and advocated for racial equality. In addition to influencing broader societal changes, the movement was also responsible for the quest of economic equality. The Civil Rights Act of 1964 was one piece of legislation that was enacted with the intention of eliminating racial discrimination and segregation in the workplace, thus contributing to a more equitable and inclusive economic environment.

Crisis in the Oil Industry and Economic Obstacles in the 1970s and 1980s:

The 1970s were characterized by a number of economic difficulties, including two oil crises that resulted in an increase in the cost of energy and a decline in economic activity. In addition, this age was witness to the transition from a manufacturing-based economy to one that is focused on providing services, the advent of globalization, and the difficulties that were brought about by deindustrialization. Through the implementation of tax cuts and deregulatory policies, President Ronald Reagan's economic policies of the 1980s attempted to encourage economic growth.

The Information Age and the Technological Revolution (roughly the 1980s to the 2000s):

The late 20th century and the early 21st century witnessed the beginning of the Information Age, which was characterized by the rapid growth of technology, the rise of the internet, and the spread of digital technologies. In this era, industries, communication, and commerce saw significant transformations, which resulted in the development of a globalized and interconnected world. Both the nature of employment and business were fundamentally altered as a result of the dot-com boom that occurred in the 1990s and the numerous technological breakthroughs that followed.

The crisis and recession that engulfed the entire world in 2008 and 2009:

There were economic difficulties at the beginning of the 21st century, the most notable of which being the Global Financial Crisis of 2008. The severe economic downturn that followed the collapse of major financial institutions, the decline in the housing market, and the accompanying recession all had far-reaching implications. Significant government interventions, such as bailouts and stimulus packages, were implemented as a result of the crisis in order to stabilize financial markets and stimulate economic recovery.

At the present time, the contemporary economic landscape is as follows:

The current economic landscape is defined by opportunities and challenges that are constantly shifting and evolving. Concerns such as income inequality, disruptions caused by technological advancements, and the influence of global events, such as the COVID-19 pandemic, continue to have an effect on the dynamics of the economy. As the United States of America navigates the complexity of the 21st century, debates on fiscal policy, trade relations, and the role of government in the economy continue to be major themes.

Resilience, adaptability, and evolution are the three main themes that can be found throughout the history of the United States economy. The economic landscape of the United States has been defined by a succession of transformative milestones that have occurred throughout its history, beginning with its colonial beginnings and culminating in its current position as a worldwide economic superpower. By looking at these significant times, we are able to acquire a more in-depth comprehension of the factors that have played a part in shaping the nation's economic identity and in determining its position in the world. The story is still being told, and each new chapter adds a new chapter to the continuous narrative of the United States of America as it navigates the problems and opportunities presented by the contemporary economic landscape.

1.2 Comparison to past economic downturns

Downturns in the economy have always been an integral part of the global economic landscape, and they have had a significant impact on the lives of individuals as well as the course that nations have taken. In the process of analyzing the current state of the economy, it is essential to make comparisons and contrasts with previous economic downturns in order to gain an understanding of the processes that are at play and to derive significant lessons for the future.

Between 1929 and 1939, the Great Depression:

When compared to other severe economic downturns, the Great Depression serves as a comparison point. There was widespread unemployment, widespread poverty, and a fall in industrial productivity as a result of this event, which was triggered by the stock market crash of 1929. Numerous factors contributed to the underlying causes, which included speculative trading, failed banking institutions, and an insufficient level of effective government action. The lessons that may be learned from this time period highlight the significance of regulatory measures to avoid excessive financial spending as well as the requirement for a stronger social safety net.

Oil Crisis (1973-1975): The Oil Crisis

During the 1970s, the world economy was confronted with the oil crisis, which was defined by the sudden and dramatic increase in the price of oil as a result of geopolitical developments in the Middle East. Stagflation, which is characterized by excessive inflation and a lack of economic growth, was brought about as a result of this crisis. During this time period, the vulnerability of economies that are heavily dependent on oil was brought to light, as was the necessity of diversifying available energy sources. A response was provided by governments in the form of monetary and fiscal measures in order to combat inflation and encourage economic growth.

During the years 2000-2002, the dot-com bubble burst

With the turn of the millennium came the bursting of the dot-com bubble, which was characterized by the failure of a great number of businesses that were founded on the internet. The stock market went through a significant downturn, which had an impact not only on technology stocks but also on the market as a whole. The events that followed brought to light the importance of employing prudent investment techniques, doing exhaustive due diligence, and making an accurate evaluation of market valuations. Additionally, throughout this time period, the groundwork was established for regulatory modifications to address issues pertaining to corporate governance.

During the years 2007-2009, the global financial crisis:

The Global Financial Crisis (GFC), which was caused by the collapse of the subprime mortgage market in the United States, was the most recent major economic downturn that occurred previous to the current era. The immense burden that was placed on financial institutions ultimately resulted in a worldwide recession. Among the lessons that can be learned from the Global Financial Crisis are the significance of cautious risk management, the necessity of stronger financial regulation, and the requirement of coordinated international measures in order to stabilize the market.

At the moment, the economic downturn:

In comparison to previous crises, the contemporary economic downturn, which is being driven by the COVID-19 epidemic, possesses a number of distinguishing traits. A health crisis, disruptions in supply chain operations, and extraordinary actions by the government are all elements that come together in this one-of-a-kind situation. This crisis, in contrast to previous economic downturns, resulted in widespread lockdowns and travel restrictions, which had a significant impact on markets like the lodging industry, tourism, and the entertainment industry.

Responses from the Government:

The recent economic downturn prompted governments all across the world to respond by implementing major fiscal stimulus packages, making modifications to monetary policy, and launching immunization drives. In contrast to the austerity measures that were put into place in the wake of the global financial crisis, the unprecedented extent of government intervention was undertaken with the intention of preventing a contraction that would be both severe and protracted. When it comes to the success of these initiatives, economists continue to argue over whether or not they were successful.

Technology advancements and working from a remote location:

The modern economic landscape is characterized by a number of important characteristics, including the rapid adoption of technology and the widespread acceptance of working remotely.

In contrast to previous economic downturns, recent developments in digital technology have enabled a great number of enterprises to quickly adjust to shifting conditions. While lockdowns were in effect, the durability of online platforms, e-commerce, and digital communication technologies was an essential factor in the continuation of economic activity.

Challenges Facing the Global Supply Chain:

As a result of the present economic slump, vulnerabilities in global supply chains have been highlighted, and disruptions have had an effect on companies that are dependent on just-in-time inventory distribution systems. As a result of the crisis, the importance of diversification and resilience in supply chains was brought to light, and businesses and governments were encouraged to reevaluate their dependence on suppliers from a single source and provide domestic production with higher priority.

Take into account the social and environmental factors:

Concerns regarding social inequality and environmental sustainability were brought to light as a result of the economic collapse that was caused by the pandemic. As a result of the crisis's disproportionate impact on vulnerable groups, governments and companies were subjected to heightened pressure to redress social inequities. Additionally, there was an increasing emphasis on establishing an economy that is more sustainable and resilient, with conversations surrounding green projects and policies that are ecologically sensitive gaining traction.

When the current economic crisis is compared to previous crises, both similarities and dissimilarities are shown through the comparison. In spite of the fact that history can teach us vital lessons, each crisis is formed by the specific conditions that it encompasses. The difficulties that are currently being faced highlight the significance of adaptation, technological resilience, and the requirement for coordinated responses on a multinational scale.

As nations traverse the complexity of recovery, politicians, corporations, and individuals can draw on the experiences of the past to inform decisions and construct a more strong and equitable economic future. This can be accomplished by drawing conclusions from the past. The conversation that is already taking place about economic policy, sustainability, and social responsibility will continue to develop, which will have an effect on the path that the world will take after the epidemic.

Chapter 2

Current Economic Indicators

When it comes to offering insights into the health and performance of a nation's economy, economic indicators play a vital role in providing those insights. These indicators are relied on by policymakers, investors, businesses, and the general public in order to evaluate the current state of the economy, for making decisions based on accurate information, and for predicting future trends. In this in-depth research, we will investigate a wide range of current economic indicators, focusing on their significance, trends, and consequences for the economic landscape of the world as a whole.

Gross Domestic Product (GDP): The Gross Domestic Product (GDP) continues to be one of the most extensively utilized measures for determining the overall health of an economy. The worth of all the commodities and services that are produced inside the borders of a country over a particular time period is what it is intended to reflect. A snapshot of economic activity can be obtained by analyzing the increase or contraction of the gross domestic product (GDP), which is broken down into components such as consumption, investment, government spending, and net exports.

The shocks that were caused by the COVID-19 pandemic have gradually been absorbed by the global GDP growth, which has been recovering as of the current period. On the other hand, the rate of recovery differs from region to region, with some economies seeing significant growth while others confront obstacles connected to the ongoing epidemic, disruptions in supply chain relations, and geopolitical concerns.

Rate of Unemployment: The unemployment rate is an important indicator that reflects the percentage of the labor force that is currently without a job. It is possible that an increase in the unemployment rate is an indication of economic distress, whereas a decrease in the rate is typically connected with economic expansion. The COVID-19 pandemic had a huge impact on labor markets around the world, resulting in the loss of jobs, the implementation of furloughs, and transformations in work patterns.

According to the current circumstances, a number of countries are struggling to meet the dual task of lowering unemployment rates while also adapting to the changing dynamics of the labor market.

The employment landscape is undergoing a transformation as a result of the proliferation of remote work, shifts in job choices, and the requirement for reskilling and continuing education.

Rate of Inflation: The rate of inflation, which is the rate at which the overall level of prices for goods and services rises, is an important economic indicator that influences the purchasing power of consumers as well as the decisions they make regarding investments. The goal of central banks is frequently to achieve a particular inflation rate in order to preserve price stability.

The topic of inflation has been the subject of a great deal of discussion and attention in recent years. There have been a number of variables that have led to inflationary pressures. These issues include disruptions in supply chains, increased demand for products and services following lockdowns, and rising commodity costs. Policymakers are confronted with the challenging issue of striking a balance between concerns about inflation and the requirement to be supportive of economic recovery.

Producer Price Index (PPI) and Consumer Price Index (CPI): The Consumer Price Index (CPI) is a measure of the average change over time in the prices that urban consumers pay for a market basket of consumer goods and services. The Producer Price Index (PPI) is a measure of the change in wholesale prices. The cost of living and the purchasing power of customers are both examined from this perspective, which is quite helpful. On the other hand, the Producer Price Index is a measurement that determines the average change over a period of time in the selling prices that domestic producers receive for their output.

A full assessment of inflationary pressures across the supply chain can be obtained by analyzing both the consumer price index (CPI) and the producer price index (PPI). Increasing costs for producers can eventually result in increased prices for consumers, which can have an impact on consumer spending patterns as well as for the general activity level of the economy.

Central banks employ interest rates as a tool to exert influence over the costs of borrowing money, as well as over spending and investment decisions. A decrease in interest rates often boosts economic activity by making borrowing money more affordable, whereas an increase in rates might assist in cooling an economy that has become overheated. While central banks manage the need to support recovery while limiting excessive inflation, the current economic environment features a fragile balance that is characterized by a delicate equilibrium.

The current environment of low interest rates has repercussions for a number of different industries, including the housing market, the financial industry, and consumer spending.

Savings people who are looking for returns on their investments are also faced with difficulties as a result of this.

Exports and imports are the two components that make up a nation's trade balance, which is the difference between the two elements. A positive balance, also known as a surplus, is achieved when exports are higher than imports, whereas a negative balance, also known as a deficit, is the result of imports being higher than exports. When it comes to a nation's current account, the trade balance is an essential component that plays a significant role in determining currency values and international competitiveness.

Changes in consumer behavior, disruptions brought on by the pandemic, and tensions brought on by tariffs have all had an impact on the dynamics of global trade interactions. In an effort to strengthen their resilience and lessen their reliance on particular regions, several economies are reevaluating their trade policies and supply chain strategy.

Consumer Confidence Index: The Consumer Confidence Index is a measurement of the degree of optimism that people feel about the overall state of the economy as well as their own particular financial situation. Higher levels of consumer confidence are often associated with higher levels of spending, whilst lower levels of confidence might result in consumers behaving more cautiously.

Following the COVID-19 epidemic, there has been a lack of consistency in the level of confidence displayed by consumers. A number of factors, including vaccination rates, worries about public health, and decisions on economic policy, have the potential to greatly influence consumer attitude and, as a result, economic activity.

Stock Market Performance: Stock market indices, such include the S&P 500, the Dow Jones Industrial Average, and others, are used as barometers to measure the sentiment of investors and the expectations of market participants toward the economy. Investing decisions, business finance, and wealth building are all susceptible to being influenced by stock prices, which are a reflection of the perceived value of companies.

The performance of the stock market in the current economic environment is a reflection of a complex interplay of elements, such as the profitability of corporations, interest rates, geopolitical events, and the ongoing impact of the pandemic on various industries.

Indicators of the Housing Market Indicators that pertain to the housing market, such as home prices, housing starts, and mortgage rates, offer insightful information regarding the larger economic picture. The housing market is frequently used as a leading indicator since it reflects movements in consumer confidence, employment, and interest rates.

Over the past few years, the housing market has witnessed a number of noteworthy phenomena, such as the escalation of home prices, the rise in demand for suburban and rural properties, and the difficulties associated with the affordability of housing.

The shifts in demographics, preferences for working remotely, and supply-side restrictions are the factors that are shaping these trends.

Finance Policy and the Level of Government Debt Both the level of government debt and the decisions that are made about fiscal policy play an important part in the economic recovery and stability. In the wake of the pandemic, numerous governments adopted expansive budgetary policies, which included the implementation of social support measures and stimulus packages. In order to successfully manage long-term budgetary sustainability while also assisting in the recovery of the economy, it is necessary to strike a balance.

The ever-increasing amounts of government debt give rise to concerns regarding the future tax loads, interest rates, and the capacity of governments to adequately respond to future economic crises. Policymakers are tasked with navigating these intricacies while simultaneously addressing the urgent requirements of the economy.

A thorough examination of the most recent economic data offers a nuanced comprehension of the complex web of causes that are influencing the economic landscape of the world. At a time when the globe is still in the process of recovering from the exceptional challenges provided by the COVID-19 pandemic, policymakers, corporations, and individuals are required to negotiate uncertainty and make decisions that are informed by a thorough study of economic data.

A holistic approach to economic analysis is essential, as seen by the interrelated nature of various indicators, which highlights the necessity of this method. A more thorough view of the economic environment requires a larger perspective that takes into consideration the interplay of elements such as globalization, technology improvements, and societal shifts. However, rather than focusing on particular metrics in isolation, it is vital to take this perspective into consideration.

Continuous monitoring of economic indicators is still extremely important, despite the fact that economies are constantly evolving and adapting to new situations.

When it comes to charting a road toward sustainable economic growth, resilience, and prosperity, stakeholders will be guided by the lessons learnt from the past as well as the insights obtained from current indicators.

2.1 Analysis of GDP trends

The Gross Domestic Product (GDP) is a measure of the overall economic health of a country. It is a comprehensive measure that encompasses the entire value of all the goods and services that are produced within the borders of that country over a particular time period. When it comes to the trajectory of economic growth, the efficacy of economic policies, and the overall well-being of a society, having a solid understanding of the patterns in GDP provides vital information. This analysis digs into the myriad intricacies of global GDP trends, analyzing the factors that are driving them, the problems that they face, and the consequences that they have for both the present and the future.

An Overview of the Global GDP:

As of the present moment, the economy of the entire world is characterized by a patchwork of different growth rates and recovery paths combined together. In the aftermath of the COVID-19 pandemic, the effects of the pandemic continue to have an impact on the patterns of GDP, resulting in a dichotomy between economies that have recovered strongly and those that are experiencing persistent difficulties.

The complexity of the global GDP landscape is caused by a number of causes, some of which include vaccination rates, governmental responses, disruptions in supply chain operations, and geopolitical conflicts. The nations that have been able to successfully implement vaccine efforts and economic policies that are flexible have experienced faster recoveries, while other nations are still struggling to deal with the long-term effects of the pandemic.

Disparities at the Regional Level The variances in GDP trends that occur at the regional level shed light on the myriad of challenges and possibilities that are encountered by various regions around the world. V-shaped recoveries, which are characterized by a quick rebound after a dramatic contraction, have occurred in certain places throughout the world. Others are confronted with an L-shaped scenario, in which the recuperation process is more drawn out and slower.

In Asia, for instance, economies such as China have shown amazing resilience and speedy recovery, which has contributed significantly to the expansion of the global GDP. Some European countries and rising economies, on the other hand, continue to struggle with obstacles such as sluggish vaccination rollouts, new COVID-19 strains, and geopolitical uncertainty throughout the world.

Trends in GDP are inextricably tied to sectoral dynamics, which reflect shifts in consumer behavior, technical improvements, and global demand patterns. Sectoral dynamics are a reflection of these shifts. The pandemic-related restrictions had a significant impact on the service industry, which included the hospitality, tourist, and entertainment industries. As a result, the sector saw severe contractions. In the meantime, fields such as technology, e-commerce, and healthcare have emerged as robust industries that have been generating economic activity despite the challenges they have faced.

Sectoral contributions to GDP were significantly influenced by the degree to which industries were able to adapt to the change brought about by digital transformation. Nations that have economies that are varied and have solid technological underpinnings have shown better resilience, highlighting the need for economic diversity and innovation in maintaining prosperity.

Problems with the Supply Chain Disruptions in global supply networks have caused reverberations throughout economies, hurting output, commerce, and overall GDP growth. As a result of the pandemic, vulnerabilities in just-in-time inventory systems were brought to light, which made it necessary to reevaluate supply chain tactics. The manufacture and distribution of commodities have become more complicated as a result of shortages of critical components, delays in shipping, and increasing transportation costs, which has had an effect on the patterns of the US gross domestic product.

In the present moment, nations are reassessing their dependence on particular suppliers and investigating various methods to improve the resilience of their supply chains. Initiatives to regionalize or localize supply chains, in conjunction with investments in digital technologies such as blockchain, are aimed at mitigating risks and bolstering economic stability.

Government Responses and Fiscal Policies: In order to mitigate the pandemic's impact on the economy, governments all over the world have implemented a variety of fiscal policies. There has been a significant amount of assistance provided to people and businesses through the implementation of infrastructural expenditures, social support programs, and stimulus packages. Different countries have experienced varying degrees of success with these measures in terms of their ability to stimulate demand, prevent bankruptcies, and maintain jobs.

The difficulty lies in striking a balance between the requirement for ongoing support and the preservation of long-term financial viability. It is possible for inflationary pressures, higher interest rates, and future economic issues to result from excessive government expenditure in the absence of a well-defined plan for economic recovery and debt management.

Increased Inflationary Pressures: Inflation, a significant factor that determines the patterns of GDP, has become more prominent in talks about the economy. Increasing inflationary pressures have been brought about by a confluence of causes, including but not limited to growing demand, disruptions in supply chain operations, and rising commodity costs. When it comes to controlling interest rates, central banks are faced with the challenging goal of containing inflation while simultaneously fostering economic recovery.

Inflation that persists over time can reduce the purchasing power of consumers, which in turn can have an effect on consumption patterns and overall GDP growth. For the purpose of preventing the economy from overheating while also supporting sustainable growth, policymakers need to strike a delicate balance.

In the context of the pandemic, technological developments have played a significant impact in shaping Gross Domestic Product trends. This is especially true in the context of technological resilience and innovation. The capacity of firms to transition to digital platforms, to accept remote employment, and to adopt creative solutions has been an essential component of economic resilience. In order to overcome economic obstacles and capitalize on emerging opportunities, nations that engage in research and development, technology infrastructure, and digital literacy are in a better position to do so.

The digital divide, on the other hand, continues to be a cause for worry since different levels of access to and expertise with technology can exacerbate existing economic inequities. For the purpose of bridging these gaps and ensuring a technology landscape that is more inclusive and sustainable, policymakers and businesses need to work together.

ESG, or environmental, social, and governance, considerations include the following:

The trends of the gross domestic product are being examined more and more through the perspective of environmental sustainability, social responsibility, and good governance. On the international scene, there has been a growing awareness of the critical nature of tackling climate change, developing social fairness, and fostering transparent governance processes. Companies and nations that prioritize environmental, social, and governance (ESG) principles are receiving increased attention from investors, consumers, and governments. This is due to the fact that these values have a long-term impact on economic growth and stability.

Through the alignment of economic policies with environmental, social, and governance (ESG) issues, not only are critical global challenges addressed, but economies are also positioned to be resilient and competitive in the ever-changing world.

A deeper knowledge of the complex dynamics that are driving the present economic landscape can be gained through the examination of changes in global GDP. The complexities of economic recovery and growth are highlighted by the interplay of regional differences, sectoral dynamics, supply chain issues, government actions, and technological advancements within the economy.

As nations traverse the challenges of the post-pandemic age, the lessons that have been gleaned from this analysis highlight the necessity of adaptability, innovation, and taking a holistic approach to the process of governing. It is necessary to strike a delicate balance between short-term interventions and long-term planning in order to achieve sustainable economic growth. Additionally, it is essential to have a great awareness of environmental and social problems.

The trajectory of global GDP trends is dependent on the capacity of nations to cultivate economic practices that are both inclusive and sustainable, to create resilience, and to embrace technological advancements in a responsible manner. When it comes to achieving economic prosperity, the world is confronted with a number of problems and opportunities that will have a significant impact on the future for future generations.

2.2 Unemployment rates and labor market challenges

Rates of unemployment and the dynamics of the labor market are important indicators that reflect the robustness and health of an economy. Beyond the realm of simple statistical data, these measurements offer a look into the experiences that individuals and communities actually go through in their daily lives. This analysis investigates the complex nature of unemployment rates and the issues that are encountered by labor markets. It discusses the causes that are at the root of these challenges, the impact that global events have had, and the various solutions that may be implemented to solve these challenges.

One of the Most Important Economic Indicators: Unemployment Rates

In order to determine the health of labor markets, it is essential to consider unemployment rates, which are stated as a proportion of the workforce that is currently without employment. They encompass both cyclical and structural components of the economy, reflecting oscillations in the demand for labor and the ability of individuals to find employment that is appropriately suited to their skills and interests.

There is a correlation between a high unemployment rate and economic suffering, which can contribute to societal problems such as poverty and inequality of opportunity. On the other hand, chronically low unemployment rates might result in a lack of available skills, wage pressures, and possibly inflationary problems. Achieving a state of continuous economic well-being requires that the appropriate equilibrium be achieved.

In order to have a comprehensive understanding of the complexities of unemployment, it is necessary to investigate the various varieties of unemployment, each of which has its own unique causes and ramifications.

In the event that persons are in the process of shifting between occupations, they are considered to be experiencing frictional unemployment. During times when people are looking for better possibilities or making changes in their careers, it is frequently regarded as a natural and transient part of the labor market.

Structural Unemployment: This type of unemployment is caused by modifications to the

economy that occurs over a longer period of time, such as developments in technology, industry reorganization, or changes in consumer preferences. Because of this sort of unemployment, initiatives to retrain and reskill workers are required in order to bring the workforce into alignment with the changing demands.

Cyclical unemployment is a type of unemployment that is linked to economic cycles. This type of unemployment occurs during economic downturns, when demand for goods and services decreases, which results in decreased output and people being laid off from their jobs. When it comes to addressing cyclical unemployment, it is common practice to deploy economic recovery initiatives and stimulus measures.

Seasonal unemployment: This type of unemployment is linked to fluctuations in demand that are caused by seasonal variables. There is a possibility that certain seasons of the year will cause employment levels to fluctuate in certain industries, including agricultural, tourism, and retail shopping.

The impact of global events on unemployment rates can be significant. Some examples of global events that can have a significant impact on unemployment rates include economic recessions, financial crises, and pandemics. The COVID-19 pandemic is the most recent and significant example of this phenomenon. It caused broad disruptions across businesses, which resulted in the loss of jobs, furloughs, and changes in work habits.

A number of developments, including remote work, digitalization, and automation, were accelerated as a result of the pandemic, which presented the labor market with both obstacles and opportunities. While certain industries, such as technology and online commerce, showed signs of expansion, others were confronted with difficulties that had never been seen before. The disparate effects that global events have on various sectors of the economy highlight the importance of implementing labor market policies that are both flexible and inclusive.

Disruptions in the Labor Market caused by Rapid Technological breakthroughs Rapid technological breakthroughs, such as artificial intelligence, automation, and robots, are changing labor markets all over the world. Despite the fact that these technologies enable higher productivity and creativity, they also present obstacles in the form of the displacement of specific jobs and the requirement of new skill sets.

The topic of discussion around the "future of work" is on the necessity of continuous upskilling and reskilling in order to guarantee that our workforce will continue to be able to adapt to the ever-changing technological landscape. It is imperative that governments, corporations, and educational institutions work together to close the skills gap and better educate workers for the opportunities that will be available in the future.

The changing nature of work, including telecommuting and the gig economy:
Traditional conceptions of the workplace were altered as a result of the COVID-19 epidemic, which increased the adoption of employees working from home. Remote work raises issues about work-life balance, mental health, and the possible loss of corporate culture. While it does give flexibility and access to a larger talent pool, it also raises concerns about what happens to the culture of the company.

There has been a rise in the prevalence of the gig economy, which is defined by labor arrangements that are both short-term and freelance. Even though it gives workers more flexibility, it also raises concerns about the safety of their jobs, the benefits they get, and their rights as workers. It is a significant problem for those who are responsible for formulating policies on the labor market to find a middle ground between the benefits of flexible work arrangements and the requirement for worker rights.

Globalization and Outsourcing: Globalization has made it easier for people to relocate their jobs across international borders, which has led to an increase in the number of jobs that are left offshore or outsourced. Despite the fact that this has helped firms become more cost-efficient, it has also resulted in the loss of jobs in a number of different industries and locations. Globalization presents policymakers with a tough challenge: they must strike a balance between the benefits of globalization and the necessity to address issues like job displacement and inequality.

Demographic Shifts and Aging Workforces: The labor markets are facing extra issues as a result of demographic shifts, which include the aging of populations in many developed nations. The workforce is getting older, which might result in a lack of skilled workers, higher healthcare expenditures, and strains on pension administration systems.

In order to maintain economic productivity, it is essential to have policies in place that both encourage older people to participate in the labor and handle the requirements of a workforce that includes members of many generations.

Skills Mismatches in the Labor Market and Educational Disparities The disparities in educational access and quality are a contributing factor to the skills mismatches that exist in labor markets. It is possible that certain regions and demographic groups may not have access to quality education and training programs, which contributes to the perpetuation of inequality and the worsening of unemployment. Taking action to address these discrepancies through the implementation of specific educational programs and vocational training initiatives is absolutely necessary in order to promote economic growth that is inclusive.

The social and economic repercussions of high and chronic unemployment rates are far-reaching and have a significant impact on the economy. In addition to experiencing a sense of detachment from the job market, those who are experiencing long-term unemployment may also endure financial difficulties and a decline in their well-being. Furthermore, high unemployment rates can put a burden on social safety nets, contribute to an increase in inequality, and impede the expansion of the economy as a whole.

Policy Responses and Future Considerations: When it comes to establishing policies to address issues related to unemployment and the labor market, governments play a key role. This involves the implementation of targeted stimulus measures during times of economic downturn, investments in education and training, support for worker transition programs, and the building of an environment that is conducive to the growth and success of enterprises.

In addition, it is vital to have policies that encourage inclusivity, diversity, and equitable chances in order to solve the systemic difficulties that are present within labor markets. When it comes to ensuring that labor practices are fair and equitable, it is of the utmost importance to take into account worker safeguards, social safety nets, and the regulation of developing kinds of employment, such as gig work.

According to the findings of the examination of unemployment rates and obstacles in the labor market, the landscape is a complex and ever-changing one that is molded by global events, technological improvements, and the dynamics of the socioeconomic system. It is necessary to take a comprehensive approach in order to successfully navigate these problems. This approach should address the various factors that contribute to unemployment, encourage adaptation among workers, and make certain that economic policies encourage growth that is both inclusive and sustainable.

Building resilient labor markets requires collaboration between policymakers, firms, and individuals. This is especially important in light of the continuous alterations in work patterns, technological disruptions, and the aftermath of the COVID-19 epidemic that the globe is currently experiencing. It is possible for societies to chart a route toward a future that is more strong, equitable, and sustainable if they encourage innovation, embrace inclusion, and invest in the skills and well-being of the workforce.

2.3 Inflationary pressures and their impact

Within the context of economics, inflation is a fundamental phenomenon that has far-reaching repercussions. Inflation is defined as the steady increase in the overall price level of goods and services over time. It is generally accepted that a healthy economy will have a modest level of inflation; however, hyperinflation, which is characterized by inflation that is both excessive and unpredictable, can present considerable issues. An investigation into the factors that lead to inflationary pressures, the effects those pressures have on different aspects of the economy, and the methods that policymakers use to control inflation are all included in this examination.

A Comprehensive Understanding of Inflationary Pressures Inflationary pressures are the outcome of a number of different variables, including demand-driven and supply-driven forces. The phenomenon known as demand-pull inflation takes place when aggregate demand exceeds aggregate supply. This results in an increase in the amount of competition for goods and services, which in turn leads to rising prices. This might be motivated by a variety of sources, including higher spending by consumers, increased spending by the government, or increased investment.

The third type of inflation, known as cost-push inflation, is caused by rising production costs, which are frequently brought about by causes such as increased wages, higher commodity prices, or disruptions in supply chain operations. When manufacturers are confronted with greater costs, they may choose to pass those costs on to customers in the form of higher pricing.

Impact on the Purchasing Power of Consumers One of the most significant effects of inflation is the decrease in the purchasing power of consumers. The same amount of money may purchase a smaller quantity of goods and services as prices continue to rise, which results in a decrease in real income. The impact of this phenomenon is most evident for persons with fixed incomes, such as pensioners who receive pensions, who may discover that their purchasing power decreases over the course of time.

Inflation has the potential to change consumer behavior, leading individuals to spend more money right away rather than putting money away for potential future expenses.

There is a possibility that this will contribute to a cycle of increased demand, which would then lead to additional inflationary pressures.

Effects on Savings and Investments: The effects of inflation on savings and investments are significant and should not be underestimated. There is a possibility that fixed-interest assets, such as savings accounts or bonds, would not keep up with inflation, which will result in a significant degradation of their value. When it comes to preserving and growing their money, investors look for returns that are higher than inflation. If they are unable to achieve this, it might discourage savings and impair the formation of capital.

Furthermore, uncertainty regarding future inflation rates might have an effect on investment decisions. This is because firms may be unwilling to make long-term commitments in an environment that is characterized by unpredictability. Due to this uncertainty, economic growth and the creation of new jobs may be hampered.

Inflation can have a number of different effects on the labor market, and these effects can be quite significant. In the event that wage increases do not keep pace with inflation, it is possible that workers will suffer a fall in their real wages, which may result in unhappiness and the possibility of labor disputes. In contrast, if wages increase at a faster rate than productivity, this might be a factor that contributes to cost-push inflation, which occurs when businesses pass on greater labor expenses to their customers.

It is still difficult for policymakers to strike a balance that assures fair remuneration for workers while also ensuring price stability. The dynamics of the labor market are inextricably tied to inflation, and this presents a problem for policymakers.

Rates of Interest and Monetary Policy: In order to control inflation, central banks employ monetary policy, namely modifications to interest rates. It is possible for central banks to raise interest rates in response to high inflationary pressures in order to curb excessive demand and reduce household expenditure. When interest rates are higher, borrowing money becomes more expensive, which in turn leads to a decrease in businesses' investments and consumer spending.

In the opposite direction, when inflation is low or when the economy is experiencing a slump, central banks may choose to cut interest rates in order to encourage borrowing, spending, and investment. The link between interest rates, inflation, and economic activity is a delicate balance that requires policymakers to give careful consideration to the situation.

Influence on Fixed-Income and Debts: The consequences of inflation can vary depending on whether the borrower is a lender or a borrower. Inflation has the potential to reduce the real value of a borrower's debt, making it more difficult for them to repay fixed-rate debts like mortgages or loans. This tendency is referred to as "debt erosion," and it has the potential to alleviate the loads of debt that are being carried by individuals and organizations.

On the other hand, considering the fact that the actual value of future repayments is unpredictable, lenders would be reluctant to give loans in an environment where inflation is prevalent. This can lead to a shortage of credit, which restricts the amount of capital that firms have access to and impedes the expansion of the economy.

The dynamics of global commerce can be affected by inflationary pressures in a single nation, which can have a domino effect on the dynamics of global trade. The possibility exists that a nation's exports will become more expensive if it experiences much higher inflation than its trading partners. This might potentially lead to a reduction in the nation's competitiveness in the worldwide market. In contrast, a nation that exports goods may experience a surge in demand if the value of its currency decreases as a result of inflation.

In a worldwide economy, where interconnection necessitates coordinated actions among nations to preserve stable trade connections, inflation management becomes an especially difficult challenge to manage.

The inflation of asset prices can show itself in a variety of asset values, including those of real estate, stocks, and commodities, in addition to the products and services that are consumed by consumers. Those who have considerable holdings in assets that are appreciating in value have a disproportionate amount of gain from asset price inflation, which can lead to wealth inequality.

A further effect of this type of inflation is the formation of financial market bubbles, which occur when the prices of assets reach levels that are not sustainable, only to collapse later. The inflation of asset prices is something that policymakers need to keep a close eye on in order to prevent systemic hazards to the financial system.

Interruptions in the Supply Chain and Inflation: In recent years, interruptions in supply chains around the world have been a factor that has contributed to the pressures of inflation. Production and distribution networks have been disrupted as a result of events like natural catastrophes, geopolitical tensions, and the COVID-19 pandemic. This has resulted in shortages and increased costs.

Disruptions in the supply chain are a contributor to cost-push inflation because they force enterprises to incur greater costs in order to acquire supplies and complete product delivery. To effectively address these disturbances, a mix of strategic planning, diversification of supply chains, and investments in resilience are required.

Expectations Regarding Long-Term Inflation The expectations that firms and consumers have regarding future inflation have a significant impact in determining the actual consequences of inflation. If people believe that prices would continue to rise, they might increase their demands for greater wages, which would contribute to cost-push inflation. In addition, while determining prices, businesses might take into account anticipated future costs, which would result in a self-fulfilling prophecy.

The long-term inflation expectations of central banks are regularly monitored and managed by these institutions since it is necessary for the maintenance of price stability to anchor these expectations at a stable level.

Inflationary forces have a significant impact on many aspects of the economy, including the purchasing power of consumers, the decisions that business owners make about investments, and the dynamics of international trade. The role of policymakers is a delicate one, as they must traverse the complicated interaction of demand-side and supply-side elements in order to achieve the correct balance between inflation and economic growth.

Therefore, it is vital to have a solid grasp of the causes and implications of inflation in order to formulate appropriate policy responses as economies continue to develop and face new problems. Given the multidimensional nature of inflation, the influence it has on all segments of society, and the necessity of coordinated actions at both the national and international levels, policymakers have a responsibility to take into consideration these factors in order to maintain sustainable economic development.

| 34 |

Chapter 3

Global Economic Factors

The economic landscape of the world is a dynamic and interconnected system that is influenced by a multitude of influences that come from different continents, different industries, and different socioeconomic settings. A complete investigation of a variety of issues, such as trade dynamics, technology breakthroughs, demographic shifts, financial markets, and environmental considerations, is required in order to gain an understanding of the intricacies of the global economy. In the course of this investigation, we will attempt to disentangle the complex web of global economic forces by analyzing both the individual effects and the collective impact that these factors have on the current status of the global economy.

Trade and Globalization: Trade is an essential component of the global economy because it encourages economic interconnectedness and enables nations to specialize in the production of goods and services in areas where they have a comparative advantage. The economic landscape has been revolutionized as a result of the liberalization of trade policy and the rise of globalization, which has made it possible for commodities, capital, and information to flow freely across international borders.

The dynamics of global trade are significantly influenced by international trade agreements, such as those established by the World Trade Organization (WTO) and regional trade pacts. While globalization has been associated with a number of issues, such as income inequality, job displacement, and geopolitical tensions, it has also been associated with the facilitation of economic growth and the decrease of poverty in many regions.

The quick rate of technology breakthroughs has been a distinguishing characteristic of the 21st century, and it has had an impact on many parts of the global economy. Digital transformation has also been a significant factor in this. The emergence of the digital age has resulted in enormous changes to the ways in which individuals communicate with one another, businesses operate, and nations compete with one another.

Industries have been revolutionized, productivity has increased, and new economic opportunities have been generated as a result of the use of digital technologies such as blockchain, artificial intelligence, and the internet of things. The digital gap, on the other hand, continues to be a problem, since it continues to impede inclusive growth due to discrepancies in technical access and capability.

Changing demographics and aging populations: The global economy is profoundly affected by demographic trends such as population growth, aging populations, and migration patterns. These demographic shifts and patterns have a significant impact on the economy. Ageing populations are causing problems in many developed countries, including labor shortages, rising healthcare expenses, and strains on social welfare systems. These problems are causing a number of obstacles.

Conversely, several emerging countries that have populations that are young are confronted with the challenge of meeting the needs of an increasing number of young people in terms of education, employment, and social services. In order to effectively manage demographic shifts, it is necessary to formulate policies that take into account the requirements of various age groups and guarantee the continuation of economic growth.

Markets for Financial Assets and Monetary Policy Financial markets are extremely important participants in the global economic system. They have a significant impact on investment, capital flows, and the prices of currencies. The Federal Reserve, the European Central Bank, and the Bank of Japan are examples of central banks that adopt monetary policies in order to regulate interest rates, manage inflation, and stabilize financial markets.

Because of the interconnected nature of global financial markets, events that occur in one region can have far-reaching repercussions on markets all over the world. Financial crises, such as the global financial crisis that occurred in 2008, highlight the significance of employing efficient regulatory frameworks and working together with international partners in order to guarantee financial stability.

Environmental Sustainability and Climate Change: Environmental concerns have become increasingly prominent in talks regarding the economy of the entire world. The effects of climate change, the depletion of resources, and the degradation of the environment all represent substantial threats to the economic stability and the well-being of society. The push for sustainability and green initiatives is causing industries to undergo a transformation, which is encouraging corporations to embrace practices that are ecologically friendly and governments to develop legislation that alleviate the dangers associated with climate change.

Not only are the transition to a low-carbon economy and the development of renewable energy sources imperatives for the preservation of the environment, but they also represent economic opportunities in terms of the creation of jobs and the production of new products.

Elements Relating to Politics and Geopolitics Both the stability of the political system and the dynamics of geopolitical situations are important elements that greatly impact the conditions of the global economy. The flow of products and capital is influenced by a variety of factors, including diplomatic relations, international crises, and trade difficulties. There have been trade disputes as a result of the emergence of protectionist views in certain regions, which has had an impact on supply chains and economic cooperation.

For example, changes in leadership, geopolitical tensions, and international sanctions are all examples of geopolitical events that have the potential to introduce uncertainty, which in turn can have an effect on investor confidence and economic performance. Diplomacy that is effective and international cooperation are both necessary components in order to effectively manage geopolitical risks and to develop economic resilience.

Development of Infrastructure and Connectivity: Infrastructure is an essential component in both the process of economic development and the process of connecting people. Increasing productivity, facilitating commerce, and contributing to regional and global economic integration are all outcomes that can be achieved by investments in transportation, communication, and energy infrastructure. Infrastructure development initiatives, such as the Belt and Road Initiative, are transforming the economic geography of states and impacting trade patterns. These projects are also influencing trade patterns.

In order to achieve development that is sustainable, inclusive, and resilient, effective infrastructure planning necessitates coordination between governments, corporate sectors, and international agencies.

The global economic landscape is composed of social and cultural variables, which have a significant role in shaping consumer behavior, corporate practices, and market trends. These factors are key components of the global economic landscape. Product demand, marketing techniques, and the formation of new sectors are all influenced by societal values, cultural preferences, and demographic diversity.

To create effective international commercial operations, multinational corporations need to traverse the complexities of different cultures and the expectations of different societies. Furthermore, it is important to note that economic policies and corporate practices are influenced by social factors, such as income disparity and social justice movements.

Pandemics and Public Health: Public health disasters, like the COVID-19 pandemic, have brought to light the susceptibility of the global economy to events that are related to health. There is widespread economic instability as a result of pandemics, which can cause disruptions in supply networks and strain on healthcare systems. It is necessary for governments, international organizations, and the private sector to work together in order to coordinate their responses to health crises. This is done in order to reduce the negative effects on public health and economic stability.

The resilience of global economies is dependent on a number of factors, including investments in healthcare infrastructure, international collaboration on vaccine distribution, and readiness for any future health emergencies.

Educational Systems and the Development of Human Capital Human capital, which includes the knowledge, skills, and health of a workforce, is an essential factor in determining the level of economic success that a country achieves. Within the context of the development of human capital and the promotion of innovation, educational systems and training programs play a crucial role. When it comes to adapting to technological advances, increasing productivity, and competing in the global marketplace, nations that have robust educational systems are in a better position.

When it comes to tackling skill shortages, decreasing inequality, and fostering sustainable economic development, investments in education and measures that promote lifelong learning are absolutely necessary.

The landscape of the global economy is like a tapestry that is woven from a number of threads, each of which represents a different component that contributes to the formation of the dimensions of the global economy. The international economic system is characterized by its complexity and its dynamic nature, which is highlighted by the interconnectivity of these factors. Understanding these impacts and successfully managing them calls for a holistic strategy, in which individuals, businesses, and politicians work together to develop solutions that promote sustainable growth, inclusivity, and resilience.

The capacity to adjust to technology improvements, demographic shifts, environmental concerns, and geopolitical dynamics will be of utmost importance as the global economy continues to undergo transformations. In order to work toward a future that is characterized by economic prosperity, social equality, and environmental sustainability, the global community can work toward strengthening international collaboration, embracing innovation, and addressing societal and environmental considerations.

3.1 Examination of international trade dynamics

The current global economy is built on the foundation of international trade, which encourages economic growth, specialization, and interdependence among states. A multitude of factors, such as trade agreements, geopolitical considerations, technological breakthroughs, and market trends, all contribute to the formation of the dynamics of international trade. The purpose of this analysis is to delve into the complexities of international trade dynamics, examining the primary drivers, challenges, and the changing face of global commerce.

Agreements on Trade and International Organizations Both trade agreements and international organizations play a significant part in the process of sculpting the landscape of international trade. International trade is governed by a set of laws, tariffs, and standards that are defined by agreements such as the World Trade Organization (WTO), regional trade pacts (such as the European Union, NAFTA, and ASEAN), and bilateral trade agreements.

Through the elimination of trade obstacles, the promotion of fair competition, and the establishment of a framework for the settlement of disputes, these accords intend to make it easier for commodities and services to move freely across international borders. The intricate interaction of economic, political, and strategic issues among participating states is reflected in the agreement-making process, which includes both the negotiation and ratification of trade agreements.

Geopolitical Considerations and Trade Relations: The dynamics of international trade are significantly impacted by geopolitical variables' effect. There is a correlation between trade flows and investment decisions, and political stability, diplomatic relations, and geopolitical conflicts can all have an effect. Uncertainties can be introduced into the global supply chain and trade patterns as a result of trade disputes, sanctions, and changes in political leadership. These factors influence the global supply chain.

Countries frequently employ trade policies as instruments of diplomacy, employing trade agreements and limitations in order to accomplish their geopolitical goals. Businesses need to be able to handle shifting alliances, regulatory frameworks, and geopolitical threats in order to sustain robust global supply chains. This is because the geopolitical landscape is constantly moving.

The structure of global supply chains has experienced substantial modifications as a result of technology improvements, cost considerations, and market needs. Global production networks have also been impacted by these changes.

Businesses are able to take advantage of efficiencies and specialized capabilities when they participate in global production networks, which entail the coordination of manufacturing and assembly operations across different nations.

Supply networks are vulnerable to interruptions, which can be observed in the aftermath of catastrophes such as natural disasters, geopolitical tensions, and public health crises. In particular, the COVID-19 pandemic brought to light weaknesses in global supply chains, which in turn prompted a reevaluation of risk management systems and concerns for the regionalization or localization of manufacturing.

Technology and Electronic Commerce: The way in which enterprises participate in international trade has been completely transformed as a result of technological breakthroughs. Cross-border transactions have been made easier thanks to the proliferation of e-commerce platforms, digital payment methods, and online marketplaces, which have connected buyers and sellers all over the world. Small and medium-sized businesses (SMEs) have been able to enjoy easier participation in international trade as a result of technological advancements that have lowered the barriers to entry for these businesses.

Additionally, technologies such as blockchain are being investigated in order to improve the transparency, traceability, and safety of supply chains that are located all over the world. In light of the fact that organizations are rapidly adopting digital transformation, the landscape of international trade is continuously evolving, which highlights the significance of adaptation and innovation.

Trade in Services: Although conversations about international trade have typically been centered on the trade of products, the significance of trade in services has greatly increased in recent years. Finance, information technology, healthcare, and education are examples of the types of services that are increasingly becoming essential components of international trade. The expansion of the services sector in the context of international trade is facilitated by the movement of professionals across international borders, the provision of digital services, and the practice of outsourcing.

Further evidence of the revolutionary effect that trade in services has had on the economy of the entire world is provided by the growth of the digital economy, which is typified by telemedicine, online education, and remote work environments. It is essential for policymakers to take into consideration the importance of addressing regulatory difficulties and cultivating an environment that is conducive to the trade of services.

Relationships Between Trade Imbalances and Currency Dynamics Trade imbalances, which occur when a nation exports more products and services than it imports or vice versa, have the potential to influence the values of currencies and the stability of the global economy. It is possible for a nation's currency to appreciate or depreciate as a result of persistent trade surpluses or deficits, which can have an impact on the competitiveness of the nation's exports.

When it comes to international trade, currency dynamics, which include exchange rates and currency manipulation, are extremely important factors to take into mind. The price of imported goods, the competitiveness of exports, and the financial health of enterprises that engage in international trade are all affected by fluctuations in the value of currencies due to currency fluctuations.

As a result of the inherent risks associated with international trade, such as currency fluctuations, payment delays, geopolitical uncertainty, and credit concerns, trade finance and risk management are increasingly becoming increasingly important. The mechanisms of trade finance, which include export credit insurance, letters of credit, and trade finance instruments, are crucial tools that provide the means to manage these risks and facilitate transactions that take place across international borders.

It is essential for companies that engage in international trade to have risk management methods. These strategies should include financial hedging, diversification of markets, and extensive due diligence on trading partners. It is also the responsibility of governments and financial institutions to assist in the establishment of frameworks that are conducive to trade financing in order to guarantee the efficient operation of international trade.

Increasingly, there is a growing emphasis on sustainable and responsible trading practices. Sustainability and responsibility in trade are becoming increasingly important. The preferences of consumers, regulatory frameworks, and company strategy are all being influenced by environmental, social, and governance (ESG) factors. There is an expectation that businesses will adhere to policies that are both ethical and ecologically beneficial, and customers are increasingly basing their purchasing decisions on sustainability criteria.

Trading practices that are sustainable comprise reducing the negative effects on the environment, ensuring that fair labor practices are followed, and making a contribution to the social development of the countries that are involved in the supply chain. Certifications, such as organic labeling and Fair Trade certifications, are becoming increasingly popular as markers of good business practices across the industry.

Intellectual Property and Innovation: The safeguarding of intellectual property rights is an essential component of international commerce, particularly in sectors that are driven by technological advancement and innovation. Strong intellectual property frameworks, such as patents, trademarks, and copyrights, provide an incentive for innovation and ensure that firms are able to reap the benefits of their creative endeavors.

However, this might result in disagreements and difficulties in the enforcement of rights due to the fact that different nations have different legislation regarding intellectual property. When it comes to trade negotiations, considerations on intellectual property protection are frequently included. This reflects the necessity of adopting a balanced strategy that simultaneously supports innovation and addresses concerns regarding the public interest.

Pandemics and Concerns Regarding Global Health Pandemics and other emergencies affecting global health, like the COVID-19 pandemic, can have significant repercussions for worldwide trade. The pandemic caused disruptions in supply chains, brought about changes in consumer behavior, and spurred a reevaluation of risk management measures based on the findings. There was an influence on the flow of commodities and people as a result of movement restrictions, border closures, and public health interventions, which highlights the interconnection of trade and public health.

Increasing the resilience of global supply chains, investing in healthcare infrastructure, and coordinating worldwide responses to health catastrophes are some of the topics that have been brought up as a result of the pandemic experience.

Various economic, political, technological, and societal elements all contribute to the formation of the dynamics of international trade, which create a complex and comprehensive system. Understanding the complexities of global trade and being able to navigate them effectively is vital for individuals, corporations, and politicians alike as the world continues to grow more intertwined throughout the years. For the purpose of tackling issues, capitalizing on opportunities, and cultivating a global economy that is both sustainable and inclusive, adaptability, creativity, and joint efforts are of all-important importance.

The trajectory of the global marketplace will be determined by the focus placed on fair and responsible trading practices, sustainable development, and resilience in the face of global difficulties. This will be the case as international trade continues to undergo transformation. Nations have the power to exploit the benefits of international commerce in order to foster economic progress, shared prosperity, and a more interconnected world if they embrace the principles of collaboration, transparency, and adaptation.

3.2 Global economic shifts affecting the U.S. economy

The global economy is in a state of perpetual flux, which is molded by a myriad of factors ranging from geopolitical events and trade dynamics to technological improvements and environmental considerations. These considerations are all contributing aspects. These changes in the global economy have a significant impact on the United States of America because of its position as a major actor on the international economic stage. This analysis investigates the primary reasons that are contributing to shifts in the global economy and investigates the influence that these factors have on the economy of the United States.

International Trade Relations and Global Supply Chains: Trade relations are one of the key avenues via which changes in the global economy have an effect on the economy of the United States. As a result of the enormous trade that the United States engages in with countries all over the world, any interruptions or changes that occur in the global trade landscape can have significant effects.

Global supply chains, which are vital for the manufacturing and delivery of goods, are susceptible to a variety of circumstances, including geopolitical conflicts, trade agreements, and disruptions in supply chain operations. Trade disputes, shifts in tariff policy, and disruptions in key trading partners are all examples of events that have the potential to impact the cost of imports and exports. This, in turn, can have an effect on the competitiveness of firms in the United States and on the prices that consumers pay.

International Relations and Geopolitical Developments: Both geopolitical events and diplomatic relations have the potential to bring uncertainties that have an impact on the stability of the global economy and, as a result, the economy of the United States. It is possible for the dynamics of international trade to be altered by shifts in geopolitical alliances, trade agreements, and diplomatic disputes, which can have an effect on enterprises in the United States that are active in the global arena.

As an illustration, alterations in the relationship between the United States and China, the Brexit, or wars in crucial regions might have direct repercussions for the exports of the United States and the competitiveness of American firms. It is essential to engage in strategic engagement and effective diplomacy in order to successfully navigate these political upheavals and minimize the negative impact on the economy of the United States.

The competitiveness of the United States economy in the international market is significantly influenced by currency values and exchange rates. These factors play a significant role in developing the economy of the United States.

Changes in the value of the United States dollar in comparison to other currencies have an effect on the dynamics of export and import relationships. A stronger dollar can make exports from the United States more expensive for purchasers from other countries, which could lead to a decrease in exports. On the other hand, it can make imports more inexpensive for consumers in the United States.

In the opposite direction, a lower United States dollar can improve export competitiveness, but it may also result in higher import costs. In order to maintain a competitive export environment while avoiding excessive volatility, the regulation of currency rates demands a careful balance to be maintained simultaneously.

The rapid rate of technical improvements has been a driving force behind global economic shifts. Digital transformation has also been a driving force behind these shifts. As a technical leader, the United States of America is not only a contributor to these transformations but also a benefit of both of them. Various industries have been changed, business models have been altered, and the nature of work has been redefined as a result of the digital transition.

The United States technology sector is at the forefront of defining global trends and affecting economic dynamics for the reason that global marketplaces are becoming increasingly dependent on digital technologies. Nevertheless, the transformative effects of technology also present obstacles, such as the possibility of job displacement and the requirement for ongoing skill enhancement in order to keep a workforce that is as competitive as possible.

Considerations Regarding the Environment and Sustainability The concept of environmental sustainability is being recognized as a significant issue that is affecting movements in the global economy. The shift to a green economy, which is being pushed by worries about climate change and the depletion of resources, has ramifications for manufacturing businesses all around the world. Changing consumer tastes, shifting regulatory policies, and worldwide attempts to address environmental concerns all have the potential to have an impact on the United States of America, which is a key economic player.

There is the potential for the transition toward sustainable methods to have an impact on a wide variety of industries, including agriculture, manufacturing, transportation, and energy. The ripple effects of these developments arc being seen throughout the economy of the United States, with businesses adjusting their operations to meet the ever-changing demands of consumers and regulatory frameworks.

The interconnection of the global economy and its susceptibility to unanticipated obstacles have been brought to light by public health crises, such as the COVID-19 pandemic, which provided a prime example of this interconnectedness. The epidemic caused disruptions in supply chains around the world, affected the behavior of consumers, and forced changes in work habits.

Because of its tight ties to international markets, the economy of the United States was affected by factors such as decreased demand on a worldwide scale, interruptions in supply chains, and changes in consumer tastes. As a means of negotiating the risks that are associated with the global economy, the pandemic highlighted the significance of resilience and flexibility.

Dynamics of Financial Markets Because of the interrelated nature of the globe's financial markets, developments in one region of the world can have repercussions that ripple out to other regions. There is a significant degree of sensitivity between the economy of the United States and the dynamics of the global financial market. This includes fluctuations in interest rates, currency values, and investor sentiment.

The economic conditions in the United States can be influenced by a variety of events, including

financial crises, shifts in monetary policy implemented by major central banks, and fluctuations in stock markets around the world. It is imperative that the Federal Reserve and other regulatory organizations properly manage domestic policies in order to successfully navigate the influence that global financial events have on the economy of the United States.

Changes in Demographics and Migration Patterns: Changes in demographics, such as population growth, aging populations, and migration patterns, have consequences for labor markets, consumer behavior, and other aspects of economic growth. These demographic transitions have a significant impact on the economy of the United States, which is well-known for its diversified population and its reliance on immigration.

A population that is getting older has issues that are associated with labor shortages and rising healthcare expenditures, whereas immigration contributes to the diversity of the workforce and the dynamic nature of the economy. In order to handle the repercussions of demographic shifts, the United States of America needs to modify its policies in order to strike a balance between the requirements of the labor market and the concerns of social welfare.

Intellectual Property and Trade Secrets: The protection of intellectual property (IP) is an essential component of various worldwide economic shifts, particularly for nations that are known for their innovative nature, such as the United States. The protection of intellectual property, such as patents, trademarks, and trade secrets, is absolutely necessary in order to encourage innovation and to keep a competitive edge in the international market.

Intellectual property-related trade conflicts, such as those with China, have the potential to have an effect on businesses and industries in the United States. In order to successfully navigate these issues, it is essential to find a balance between the protection of intellectual property rights and the promotion of international collaboration.

Global economic movements have contributed to conversations regarding economic inequality and social dynamics, both within nations and across borders. These talks have been sparked by the combination of economic inequality and social dynamics. The United States of America is confronted with internal difficulties that are associated with gaps in access to opportunities, job displacement, and income inequality.

It is becoming increasingly important to address domestic economic inequities since global economic developments have a variety of diverse effects on different businesses. For the purpose of promoting sustainable economic development, it is vital to have policies that strive to create inclusive growth, support education and workforce development, and address social inequities.

The economy of the United States is intricately knit into the fabric of the global economic landscape, and it is susceptible to the effect of a wide variety of factors that are not limited by national boundaries. To successfully manage these global economic transitions, the United States of America needs to demonstrate both adaptability and strategic foresight. This is because the globe is undergoing continual transformations that are driven by changes in geopolitics, technology, and society.

The issue of adapting to changing trade dynamics, geopolitical risks, and the imperatives of sustainability and technological innovation is one that policymakers, businesses, and individuals in the United States must address. Therefore, in order to position the economy of the United States to survive in a global environment that is always shifting, it is vital to have a comprehensive awareness of these global economic trends, as well as tactics that are proactive and collaborative.

Chapter 4

Political and Policy Implications

The intricate interaction between global economic movements and political dynamics has far-reaching ramifications for governments, policymakers, and individuals alike. These implications were found to be far-reaching. In light of the fact that the globe is undergoing continual transformations in trade relations, technical breakthroughs, and environmental considerations, political and policy decisions are becoming increasingly important in determining the course that economies will take. This analysis investigates the complex web of political and policy consequences that have arisen as a result of developments in the global economy. It also investigates the ways in which governments react to the difficulties and opportunities that are presented by this ever-changing environment.

The trade policies of a nation are an essential component of its economic strategy, and they are closely connected to diplomatic relations and geopolitical considerations. Trade policies are a cornerstone of a nation's economic strategy. Changes in the global economy frequently need for modifications to be made to trade policies in order to successfully navigate shifting dynamics and preserve a competitive advantage.

Nations are able to exert their economic interests through the use of trade agreements, negotiations, and conflicts as arenas. As was shown in recent trade ties between the United States and China, geopolitical tensions have the potential to push governments to reevaluate their trade policies, which may result in the imposition of tariffs, sanctions, or other trade obstacles. Diplomacy, negotiations that are successful, and strategic engagement are becoming increasingly important tools for politicians that are attempting to strike a balance between economic objectives and broader geopolitical issues.

Stability and Security in Geopolitics: The stability of geopolitical affairs is inextricably related to the success of the economy, and alterations in the global economy have the potential to impact the geopolitical landscape. Trade patterns, energy dynamics, and regional alliances are all examples of factors that have the potential to change geopolitical alliances and relationships.

The diversification of energy sources and the reduction of reliance on regions that are geopolitically sensitive are two approaches that governments are pursuing in order to improve their energy security.

As can be observed in the chase of important minerals for electronic and renewable energy technologies, the search for rare minerals and resources that are necessary for technological breakthroughs can also have an effect on the dynamics of geopolitical situations.

The concept of national security covers not just military considerations but also economic resilience and the capacity to absorb shocks to the economic system. National security is not limited to military factors alone. When it comes to their local sectors, supply networks, and key infrastructure, governments have a responsibility to take into consideration the strategic consequences of global economic movements.

Policies that encourage diversity, technological innovation, and investments in vital industries are necessary in order to guarantee the resilience of the economy. The COVID-19 pandemic brought to light the significance of ensuring the safety of important products, such as pharmaceuticals and medical supplies, and spurred a reevaluation of the vulnerabilities that exist within supply chains from the point of view of national security.

Monetary Policy and Central Bank Strategies: When it comes to responding to movements in the global economy, central banks assume a pivotal role through the implementation of monetary policy programs. Central banks use a variety of methods to regulate inflation, stabilize financial markets, and affect economic growth. These instruments include changes in interest rates, quantitative easing, and currency interventions.

Within the context of a globalized economy, the monetary policies of major central banks, such as the Federal Reserve of the United States of America, the European Central Bank, and the Bank of Japan, have the potential to have adverse consequences on other countries. In order to prevent the global financial markets from becoming unstable, it is vital for central banks to coordinate their efforts and communicate with one another.

Technology Policy and Innovation Strategies: As technology continues to alter sectors and economies, governments are required to establish policies that encourage innovation, assure digital inclusion, and address the societal effects of technical advancements. There are a number of concerns that need to be carefully considered, including data privacy, cybersecurity, and the ethical application of artificial intelligence.

In addition, trade dynamics and technology policy overlap, as seen by the arguments that take place about the protection of intellectual property and the transfer of technology.

When it comes to resolving concerns of market competitiveness and the influence of tech giants, governments need to find a way to strike a balance between fostering innovation and protecting national interests.

The urgency of solving environmental concerns and mitigating climate change has pushed nations to adopt policies that encourage sustainability and environmental stewardship. These policies are referred to as environmental and climate policies. In order to make the transition to a low-carbon economy, regulatory frameworks, investments in renewable energy, and international cooperation are all necessary components.

Changes in the global economy are having an impact on the way that environmental policies are heading, and governments are confronted with the task of striking a balance between economic growth and environmental sustainability. When it comes to migrating to environmentally friendly technology, managing climate-related risks, and ensuring a just transition for affected industries and communities, policymakers have the responsibility of navigating the complexity involved.

Policies Regarding Healthcare and Public Health Emergencies in public health, such as pandemics, highlight the significance of having strong policies regarding healthcare and public health. Investing in healthcare infrastructure, research, and emergency preparedness are all areas that governments need to prioritize in order to protect their citizens and sustain economic resilience.

The COVID-19 pandemic brought to light the linked nature of global health and the necessity of international collaboration in the management of health crises. It is essential for a nation to have policies in place that address the distribution of vaccines, access to healthcare, and readiness for pandemics in order to effectively respond to global health concerns.

Policies for Social and Economic Inclusion Because movements in the global economy have the potential to increase social inequities and disparities, policymakers are required to adopt policies that are inclusive and that address the requirements of a wide range of communities. When it comes to providing residents with the skills they need to remain competitive in an economy that is always changing, education and workforce development programs become indispensable instruments.

Social and economic inclusion can be improved by the implementation of policies that encourage the provision of social safety nets, cheap housing, and access to healthcare.

When it comes to addressing the social implications of economic developments, maintaining social cohesion, and ensuring that the advantages of economic progress are distributed fairly, governments have a responsibility to take the initiative.

When it comes to economic growth and global competitiveness, investments in infrastructure are very necessary. Connectivity and infrastructure development are also critically important. Increasing a nation's productivity and making it easier for it to participate in global markets can be accomplished through the implementation of policies that pertain to the development of infrastructure, which includes transportation, energy, and digital connectivity.

In order to show the significance of infrastructure in determining geopolitical and economic impact, initiatives such as China's Belt and Road Initiative have been implemented. It is imperative that governments give priority to infrastructure projects that contribute to economic growth, regional connectivity, and resilience to shocks from the outside world.

Policies regarding education and the workforce: In order to accommodate the rapid growth of technology and the shifting economic landscape, it is necessary to have a workforce that is both skilled and flexible. The policies that govern education and the workforce are extremely important in terms of preparing citizens for the jobs of the future and decreasing the skill gaps that exist.

Investing in educational systems that encourage creative thinking, critical thinking, and technology literacy is something that governments ought to undertake. A resilient labor market that is able to navigate the obstacles provided by global economic shifts is formed via the implementation of policies that allow for flexible workforce policies and programs that encourage lifelong learning.

International Cooperation and Multilateralism: In order to effectively address the complex global challenges that we face, it is necessary to engage in multilateral methods and international cooperation. Diplomatic efforts, participation in international organizations, and adherence to agreements that promote collaboration on topics such as trade, climate change, and public health are all things that governments are required to engage in.

One of the most important factors that determines the success of global governance systems like the United Nations, the World Trade Organization, and regional alliances is the degree to which nations are willing to collaborate with one another. Policymakers are tasked with navigating the complexity of striking a balance between the imperatives of a globally interconnected world and the interests of their own nations.

There are substantial and multifaceted ramifications for politics and policy that are brought about by movements in the global economy. The difficulty of formulating policies that strike a balance between economic goals and broader factors such as geopolitical stability, environmental sustainability, and social inclusion is one that is entrusted to governments. It is imperative that policymakers demonstrate adaptability, vision, and a commitment to addressing the complex difficulties that occur as a result of the ongoing upheavals that the globe is undergoing.

A holistic strategy that takes into account the interdependence of global challenges and the necessity of international cooperation is necessary for effective governance. In order for nations to successfully traverse the ever-changing global landscape and make a contribution to a future that is more wealthy, egalitarian, and sustainable, policy frameworks should be designed to encourage resilience, inclusivity, and sustainability.

4.1 Evaluation of government policies and their impact

The policies of the government are critical instruments that are utilized for the purpose of determining the path that social development will take, overcoming issues, and pursuing national goals. The efficacy of these policies has the potential to have a significant influence on a variety of areas of a society, such as the expansion of the economy, the improvement of social conditions, the preservation of the environment, and the administration of the society as a whole. The evaluation of government policies is investigated in this analysis, which also investigates the criteria that are used to evaluate the impact of these policies and the implications for the development of society.

When examining the policies of the government, one of the most important factors to take into account is the influence those policies have on the economy. In order to maintain budgetary stability, boost economic growth, and manage inflation, policymakers frequently devise ways to accomplish these goals. When it comes to evaluating the effectiveness of economic policies, it is usual practice to utilize metrics such as the growth of the GDP, employment rates, and inflation levels.

Economic activity can be stimulated, for instance, through the implementation of fiscal policies

that include tax reforms or investments in infrastructure. In order to evaluate the impact, it is necessary to determine whether or not these policies lead to higher productivity, the development of new jobs, and an economic environment that is sustainable. On the other hand, policies that are badly developed or implemented might result in economic imbalances, unemployment, or inflationary pressures.

Well-being in Society and Equity: The policies of the government play a significant part in determining the social well-being of the population and in correcting disparities. The provision of healthcare, education, housing, and social welfare programs are all examples of social policies that are intended to improve the quality of life for the general population. Assessing access to vital services, advances in public health, educational outcomes, and general social equity are all aspects that are included in the evaluation process for this setting.

For instance, a policy on healthcare may be evaluated based on indicators such as the prevention of disease, the accessibility of healthcare, and the enhancement of the general public's health. Indicators of social well-being frequently consist of measurements of poverty rates, income distribution, and the overall level of living. These indicators offer insights on the efficiency of policies in improving the welfare of society.

Sustainability in the Environment: In this day and age, when people are becoming more aware of the environment, it is required of governments to adopt laws that encourage sustainability and reduce the negative impact that human activities have on the environment. When evaluating environmental policies, it is necessary to determine how effective they are in tackling concerns such as pollution, climate change, and the conservation of resources.

It is possible, for instance, to evaluate policies concerning sources of renewable energy, efforts to reduce emissions, and conservation activities based on the influence that these policies have on environmental indicators. The reduction of carbon emissions, the enhancement of air and water quality, and the preservation of biodiversity are all examples of metrics that could be collected. The evaluation of environmental policies is absolutely necessary in order to guarantee a balance between the development of the economy and the preservation of the environment over the long term.

There is a strong correlation between the general administration of a nation and the effectiveness of its institutions, which in turn is directly tied to the effectiveness of government policies. Both the institutions responsible for the execution of policies and the policies themselves must be capable, transparent, and accountable in order for them to be effectively executed. In the context of this discussion, evaluation entails determining the degree of corruption, as well as the efficiency of public institutions and the prevalence of corruption.

For the purpose of evaluating the efficiency of governance and institutions, various indicators are utilized. These include the ease of doing business index, the rule of law index, and corruption perception indexes. The successful implementation of policies and the general stability of a nation are both influenced by the strength of the institutions that govern it.

The opposite of strong governance is weak governance, which can impede the consequences of policy and erode public trust.

Innovation and Technological Progress: Policies enacted by the government also play a significant part in supporting innovation and technological progress. Policies that are aimed to boost a nation's competitiveness in the global scene include those that pertain to research and development, the protection of intellectual property, and investments in science and technology. As part of the evaluation process, it is necessary to determine how these policies have affected innovation ecosystems, technical breakthroughs, and the competitiveness of domestic industries.

Key factors include the amount of money spent on research and development, the number of patents that have been awarded, and the existence of a thriving ecosystem for new business ventures. Evaluating the effectiveness of innovation policies is essential for putting a country at the forefront of technical breakthroughs, which, in turn, can stimulate economic growth and improve the country's ability to compete on a global scale.

Implications for the Global Community and Diplomacy Government actions have the potential to have ramifications that extend beyond national borders, affecting diplomatic relations and the position of a nation within the international community. The impact that foreign policies, trade agreements, and international cooperation projects have on diplomatic ties, the dynamics of global trade, and the overall stability of geopolitical affairs are all factors that are taken into consideration during the review process.

Assessment of the effectiveness of policies on the international arena is accomplished through the utilization of indicators such as international trade balances, participation in global forums, and diplomatic relationships. Policies that are effective in the realm of foreign policy contribute to constructive diplomatic relations, improve the influence of a nation, and foster collaboration on topics that are internationally significant.

Perceptions of the Public and Social Harmony Both public perception and social harmony are important aspects to consider when assessing the implementation of government policy. A greater likelihood of success is associated with policies that are in line with the preferences, values, and expectations of the general population. In order to evaluate the efficacy of policies in terms of encouraging peace and meeting the expectations of the public, several methods such as public opinion polls, citizen satisfaction surveys, and social cohesion indexes are utilized.

Taking social policies that address issues of social justice, inclusion, and cultural diversity as an example, these policies may be evaluated based on measures that reflect public attitude and social cohesion. The contentment of citizens and the maintenance of social order are both influenced by policies that are viewed as being fair and inclusive.

A multidimensional process that takes into consideration a wide set of criteria encompassing economic, social, environmental, and governance dimensions, the evaluation of government policies is conducted. For the purpose of ensuring that policies favorably contribute to the development of society, policymakers are required to strike a delicate balance between policies that have opposing purposes. Policies that are effective are those that not only solve present difficulties but also align with long-term goals, thereby fostering a future that is sustainable, equitable, and prosperous.

It is essential for a comprehensive policy assessment framework to have components such as continuous monitoring, feedback systems, and adaptability. As a result of the changing nature of the global environment, governments are required to be flexible in their approach to addressing newly developing difficulties and capitalizing on opportunities to improve the well-being of their inhabitants. When it comes down to it, the evaluation of government policies acts as a compass that guides nations toward inclusive and sustainable growth in a world that is constantly shifting.

4.2 Political decisions influencing economic outcomes

It is a complicated and dynamic interplay that greatly determines the trajectory of nations, and the relationship between political actions and economic outcomes is a primary driving force behind this. Various facets of the economy, including fiscal policies, regulatory frameworks, and international trade ties, are influenced by political leaders through the process of policy formulation and implementation. This examination digs into the complex nature of political decisions and the impact they have on economic outcomes. It investigates the key mechanisms, obstacles, and implications that these decisions have for societies.

Fiscal Policies and Government Spending: The decisions that are made by the government, particularly those that are linked to fiscal policies, play a significant impact in determining the outcomes associated with the economy. There is a clear correlation between the decisions that are made about taxation, government expenditure, and budgetary allocations and the general economic health of a nation. One example of a decision that can boost economic growth is the decision to reduce taxes, which can lead to increased consumer spending and company investment.

Alternately, governmental decisions to raise taxes may have an effect on the amount of discretionary spending that consumers have and the profits that businesses make, which may result in a slowdown of economic activity. It is possible for decisions made by the government regarding expenditures on infrastructure, healthcare, and education to have long-term effects on the economy. These decisions can have an impact on productivity, workforce skills, and the overall competitiveness of a company or nation.

Monetary Policies and the Independence of Central Banks: Political decisions extend to monetary policies, which are the means by which governments exert influence over inflation, money supply, and interest rates through the use of central banks. When it comes to ensuring that monetary policies are effective, the independence of central banks is an essential component. This independence enables choices to be made primarily on economic factors rather than on short-term political goals.

It is possible for political meddling in monetary policy to result in inflationary pressures and to undermine the long-term stability of the economy. One example of this is when central banks are pressured to undertake expansionary measures in order to secure electoral advantages. On the other hand, monetary policies that are properly calibrated have the potential to contribute to price stability, low inflation, and an environment that is conducive to the growth of the economy in a sustainable manner.

The regulatory frameworks that control company operations, commerce, and financial markets are shaped by political decisions. The business environment is also influenced by these regulatory frameworks. By streamlining laws, lowering bureaucratic impediments, and cultivating a climate that is conducive to commercial competition, pro-business policies have the potential to encourage entrepreneurial endeavors and boost investment opportunities.

On the other hand, strict laws, bureaucratic inefficiency, and unpredictable policy changes can discourage corporate operations and impede the growth of the economy. When it comes to guaranteeing regulatory monitoring and fostering an atmosphere that supports innovation, competitiveness, and job creation, political leaders have the responsibility of navigating the delicate balance that exists between the two.

Trade Policies and Global Economic Relations: The decisions that are made by politicians about trade policies have far-reaching repercussions on the economic outcomes of a nation. The participation of a nation in the global economy is impacted by a variety of factors, including trade agreements, tariffs, and diplomatic ties. There is the potential for a nation's industries, jobs, and overall competitiveness to be influenced by decisions regarding whether or not to engage in free trade agreements or to adopt protectionist policies.

For instance, a decision to impose tariffs on imports may benefit domestic businesses, but it may also result in retaliatory actions and disruptions in supply networks around the world. The adoption of free trade agreements, on the other hand, has the potential to expand market access, boost exports, and bring about greater economic integration. When it comes to trade issues, political leaders need to negotiate them carefully in order to strike a balance between home interests and the requirement of global economic cooperation.

Investment Climate and Foreign Direct Investment: The decisions that are made by political leaders have a substantial impact on the investment climate and, as a result, the flow of foreign direct investment (FDI). Policies that encourage a political environment that is stable, safeguard property rights, and preserve the rule of law have the potential to attract financial investors from other countries who are looking for a business environment that is secure and predictable.

On the other hand, political instability, corruption, and inconsistent policies can be factors that discourage foreign investment and impede economic progress. Countries that have favorable investment climates typically see greater capital inflows, increased exchange of technology, and increased job creation, all of which contribute to the general economic development of the country.

Policies pertaining to the labor market and the dynamics of the workforce: Political decisions concerning labor market policies, such as minimum wage laws, workplace restrictions, and social welfare programs, have an effect on the dynamics of the workforce and the outcomes of the economy respectively. There is a potential for economic efficiency and productivity to be increased through the implementation of policies that strike a balance between protecting the rights of workers and encouraging a flexible labor market.

In addition, decisions about investments in education and the development of skills have an impact on the quality of the workforce as well as its adaptability to shifting economic demands. In order to develop a labor market that is both harmonious and dynamic, political leaders are faced with the difficulty of tackling issues such as unemployment, income inequality, and workforce participation.

Income Redistribution and Social Welfare Programs: The decisions that are made by politicians regarding social welfare programs and income redistribution policies have direct repercussions for the outcomes of the economy and the well-being of society. Policies that combat poverty, offer social safety nets, and encourage inclusiveness all contribute to the maintenance of social order and have the potential to boost economic output from a broader perspective.

However, in order to avoid unexpected consequences such as disincentives to labor or fiscal imbalances, it is necessary to give serious consideration to the design and implementation of social welfare programs. When it comes to tackling social disparities and sustaining economic incentives for growth, political leaders are required to navigate the trade-offs that exist between the two.

Environmental Policies and Sustainable Development: In light of the environmental difficulties that are being faced on a worldwide scale, political decisions concerning environmental policies are becoming an increasingly important factor in determining the consequences of economic activities. Regulatory frameworks and financial incentives that are designed to encourage environmentally responsible practices, reduce the effects of climate change, and guarantee environmental stewardship have the potential to impact industry, innovation, and resource management.

It is possible that nations that embrace environmentally conscious policies that are forward-thinking will reap the benefits of developing green industries, the creation of jobs in renewable energy sectors, and increased resilience to environmental hazards. On the other hand, political decisions in this area frequently involve making difficult choices between the protection of the environment and the expansion of the economy.

Considerations & Obstacles to Overcome:

Both short-term and long-term goals are important

Election cycles frequently have an impact on political decision-making, and these cycles may give more weight to short-term advantages than they do to long-term goals. The problem for policymakers is to find a way to strike a balance between the imperative of sustainable economic development and the urgent political factors that are at play.

Interconnectedness that is Complicated:

Because of the complexity and interconnectedness of economic systems, it is difficult to accurately forecast the all-encompassing effects that political decisions will have. The assessment of the effects of policy can be made more difficult by the presence of unintended consequences and spillover effects that extend beyond industries and borders.

Implementation of New Policies:

One of the most important factors that determines the efficacy of political decisions is not only the formulation of policies but also the successful execution of those policies.

The influence that well-conceived programs are supposed to have can be undermined by bureaucratic inefficiency, corruption, and a lack of enforcement measures.

Relations of Interdependence and Globalization:

During this age of globalization, political actions made in one nation might have repercussions in other nations around the world. In order to effectively address the interconnected nature of trade relations, financial markets, and supply chain dynamics, policymakers need to adopt a sophisticated strategy that takes into account the ramifications of both domestic and foreign factors.

The perception of the public and the political will:

Political decisions are significantly influenced by both the public's perception and the political will of the people present. Public sentiment, which is affected by the media, advocacy groups, and social values, can have an effect on the willingness of political leaders to embrace particular policies, even if those policies are environmentally and economically sound.

One of the most important factors in the growth of nations is the complicated and multifaceted relationship that exists between political actions and the outcomes of economic developments. In order to successfully navigate a complex environment, policymakers need to take into account the varied interests of a wide range of stakeholders and strike a balance between short-term political considerations and long-term economic goals.

The decisions that are effective in politics are those that create an environment that is favorable to the growth of the economy, innovation, and the general well-being of society. A dedication to good governance, policymaking that is evidence-based, and a deep knowledge of the interconnectivity of economic systems in a world that is continuously changing are all necessary components for striking the proper balance. In the end, the prosperity and trajectory of societies on a global scale are determined by the synergy that exists between the decisions made by political leaders and the consequences of economic activities.

Chapter 5

Societal Consequences

There are significant ramifications for societies as a result of the complicated dance that takes place between political actions and economic outcomes. Communities are influenced in terms of their well-being, possibilities, and dynamism by the complexity of the tapestry that is created by the intersection of politics and economics. Through the examination of the effects that the interaction of political and economic forces has on individuals, communities, and larger social institutions, this approach investigates the myriad of societal repercussions that have arisen as a result of this interaction.

The formation and continuation of income inequality is one of the ubiquitous societal implications that are a result of the dynamics of the political and economic systems. Social stratification is another consequence of these dynamics. The distribution of wealth within a society is influenced by political decisions, such as those pertaining to tax laws and regulations governing the labor market. The consequences of the economy, which are driven by variables such as globalization and technological improvements, have the potential to either increase or reduce variations in income.

Income disparity has far-reaching repercussions, including a negative impact on prospects for upward mobility, access to education and healthcare, and general access to these resources. Increasing the disparity between those who are wealthy and those who are marginalized can be a factor in the stratification of society, which in turn can lead to differences in living standards and a reduction in social cohesion.

There is a strong correlation between political decisions regarding education policies and funding and the disparities that exist in the educational system. These decisions have significant repercussions for economic mobility and societal equity. Choices made by political leaders frequently have an effect on the availability and quality of educational opportunities, which in turn affects the capacity of individuals to acquire skills and participate in the labor force. There is a strong correlation between educational attainment and economic results, such as the number of job opportunities and the increase of wages.

Among the societal repercussions are the persistence of poverty that is passed down from generation to generation and, on the other hand, the ease of upward mobility.

It is possible for particular demographics to face hurdles to entrance as a result of educational differences, which in turn restricts their capacity to fully engage in the economic and social fabric of contemporary society.

Access to Healthcare and Public Health: The intersection of political decisions about healthcare policies and economic considerations, such as income and employment, has an effect on the results of public health. The decisions that are made by political leaders have an impact on the accessibility of healthcare services, health insurance, and the overall health infrastructure. Individuals' access to high-quality medical treatment is impacted by economic factors such as the stability of their employment and their income levels.

One example of societal implications is the existence of differences in health outcomes related to socio-economic determinants. The continuation of health disparities can be caused by a lack of access to healthcare services, which typically has a disproportionately negative impact on groups who are already marginalized. For the purpose of developing a healthcare system that contributes to the general well-being of society, it is essential to take into consideration the interaction between political decisions and economic variables.

Employment Opportunities and Job Insecurity: The decisions that are made by politicians regarding labor market policies, trade agreements, and economic regulations have a significant impact on employment opportunities and job security. The outcomes of the economy, which are influenced by factors such as globalization and technological improvements, lead to shifts in the labor market. In the realm of employment, the landscape is shaped by political decisions about worker protections, minimum wage regulations, and unemployment benefits.

Different parts of the population will experience varying degrees of job security, income stability, and overall economic resilience as a result of the societal implications. As a result of economic downturns or structural changes in industries, job displacement can occur, which could contribute to the stress that society is experiencing and could potentially expand social cleavages that already exist.

There is a clear relationship between the interaction between political actions and economic consequences, and this relationship has significant ramifications for both social cohesiveness and political stability. There are a number of factors that might contribute to social discontent and political upheaval, including economic inequality, a lack of opportunities, and perceptions of unfairness. The decisions that are made at the political level, notably those that pertain to social welfare programs and the regulation of financial markets, play a significant part in either making these tensions less severe or making them more severe.

The potential for social disintegration, polarization, and even political instability are all examples of the potentially negative effects on society. In addition to contributing to a feeling of alienation among various parts of society, the weakening of social cohesion can make it more difficult for groups to work together to find solutions to problems that are shared by all.

Cultural Dynamics and Identity: Political decisions and economic consequences are also factors that have an impact on the cultural dynamics and individual identities that exist inside societies. It is possible for cultural practices and ideals to be influenced by economic upheavals, whether they are caused by globalization or changes in industries. In addition, the mosaic of societal identity is further shaped by political decisions, such as those pertaining to immigration policies and efforts to preserve cultural traditions.

The potential for cultural tensions, identity crises, or, on the other hand, the enrichment of cultural diversity are all possibilities that are included in the societal consequences. Policymakers face a complex problem when it comes to striking a balance between the advancement of the economy and the preservation of cultural traditions. This challenge requires them to give careful attention to the repercussions that their actions will have on society.

The effects of economic results, particularly those that are driven by technical breakthroughs, have the potential to destabilize established societal structures. Social adaptation is a necessary response to these sorts of outcomes. Industry can be reshaped by technological developments such as automation, artificial intelligence, and other technical advancements, which can also change job landscapes and the skills that are required. Whether or not these transformations will have a significant impact on society is directly proportional to the political decisions that are made on the regulation of technology, education, and social safety nets.

Among the societal repercussions are the possibility of job displacement, the requirement for workforce retraining, and the rise of new social difficulties that are associated with the incorporation of technology into everyday life. Policymakers have the responsibility of navigating these developments in order to guarantee that the advantages brought about by technological advancement are dispersed fairly throughout society.

Environmental sustainability and social resilience are two concepts that are directly tied to one another. Political decisions regarding environmental policy and economic concerns related to resource management have direct effects for the resilience of society. Changes in climate, the depletion of natural resources, and the destruction of the environment are all consequences of decisions made at the political and economic levels. There is a possibility that the societal implications will include an increased susceptibility to environmental disasters, the relocation of people, and problems relating to health.

In order to effectively address these difficulties, it is necessary to utilize coordinated efforts to match political decisions with economically sustainable practices. It is imperative that proactive policies that prioritize environmental conservation and adaptation measures be implemented in order to ensure the resilience of societies in the face of ever-changing environmental conditions.

Interconnection on a Global Scale and the Exchange of Cultures An increasing number of political and economic variables are contributing to the phenomenon of global interconnection. Economic partnerships, diplomatic contacts, and trade policies all have a role in shaping the interactions that societies have with one another on the international arena. The effects for society include the exchange of cultural ideas, the exposure to a variety of points of view, and the introduction of opportunities for working together to address global concerns.

On the other hand, global interconnection also presents a number of concerns, such as the possibility of cultural clashes, economic dependency, and geopolitical confrontations. Policymakers have the responsibility of navigating these intricacies in order to capitalize on the productive benefits of global collaboration while simultaneously limiting the hazards that are associated with interconnected economic and political systems.

The interplay between political actions and economic outcomes has a wide range of outcomes that have a profound impact on society. These outcomes are enormous, intricate, and profoundly important. The task of navigating this complicated landscape in order to advance societal well-being, equity, and resilience is a responsibility that policymakers must fulfill. It is necessary to give careful consideration to the wide-ranging effects that political decisions have on individuals, communities, and larger societal structures in order to achieve a balance between the advancement of the economy and the maintenance of social cohesion.

Political leaders have the ability to contribute to the construction of societies that are prosperous economically, socially, and culturally by resolving disparities, fostering inclusivity, and placing a priority on sustainable development. The continuing conversation that takes place between political decisions and economic outcomes is an essential component in the process of constructing a future in which societies are able to adapt, flourish, and meet the challenges that come with living in a world that is constantly changing.

5.1 Impact on income inequality

There is a serious problem that has substantial ramifications for both social cohesion and economic stability, and that problem is income inequality, which refers to the disparity in earnings that exists between different parts of society. One of the most important factors that contributes to the formation of the landscape of income inequality is the complex interaction that exists between political actions and economic consequences. Through the examination of major determinants, problems, and potential paths for addressing this ubiquitous societal concern, this paper investigates the varied impact that political and economic forces have on income disparity.

Policies Regarding Taxation and the Distribution of Wealth The decisions that are made by politicians regarding taxation policies have a direct influence on the disparity in income. When it comes to the distribution of wealth, tax systems, which include progressive tax rates and the taxation of capital gains, constitute an essential component. It is possible for political decisions to either reduce or increase tax rates for various income categories, which can either reduce or worsen existing income disparities for the population.

The implementation of progressive tax systems, which impose higher rates on higher income levels, is one example of a decision that can help to a more equitable distribution of wealth. In contrast, tax cuts that disproportionately benefit the wealthy may result in a wider income disparity between the two groups. When it comes to formulating taxation policies that specifically target income disparity, it is absolutely necessary to find a middle ground between budgetary prudence and social equity.

Rules of the Labor Market and Wage gaps: Wage gaps and income inequality are influenced by political decisions that revolve around labor market rules, minimum wage laws, and workers' rights. There is a correlation between policies that promote a fair and competitive labor market and the reduction of income disparities. On the other hand, policies that reduce labor rights or fail to address discrepancies in salaries across different industries can contribute to the perpetuation of income inequality.

The implementation of proactive labor market policies that encourage fair salaries, collective bargaining, and opportunities for skill development is absolutely necessary in order to address wage discrepancies. In order to establish a labor market that is both inclusive and egalitarian, political leaders are required to manage the intricacies of striking a balance between the interests of workers and businesses.

Access to Education and Skill Development: The decisions that are made by politicians regarding education policy have a long-lasting impact on income inequality because they have an effect on the access that individuals have to quality education and the development of their skills. Education is a significant factor in determining the future earnings of an individual, and policies that guarantee equal access to educational opportunities have the potential to contribute to the reduction of income gaps.

It is possible for political decisions to have a positive impact on income mobility. Some examples of such decisions include investing in early childhood education, addressing gaps in K-12 education, and making higher education more accessible. Policymakers have the ability to address one of the fundamental causes of income disparity by acknowledging the importance of education as a method of achieving upward mobility.

Social Welfare Programs and the Alleviation of Poverty Political decisions that are related to social welfare programs play a vital role in alleviating the impact of income inequality, particularly for groups that are vulnerable. It is possible to alleviate poverty and narrow income gaps by the implementation of policies that create a comprehensive social safety net. These policies may include unemployment benefits, access to healthcare, and housing help.

On the other hand, policies that reduce the scope of social welfare programs or eliminate them entirely may have a disproportionate impact on persons with lower incomes and result in an increase in income disparity. The social repercussions of austerity measures need to be carefully considered by policymakers, and they should give those programs that provide a safety net for individuals who are experiencing economic difficulties the highest priority.

Globalization and Trade policy: The globalization of economies and the political decisions that are related to trade policy have complex ramifications for the disparity of income. In spite of the fact that globalization has the potential to result in higher economic growth, it also has the potential to cause certain portions of the workforce to experience job displacement and pay stagnation. The implementation of trade policies that give priority to environmental standards and fair labor practices can be of assistance in mitigating the adverse effects of income disparity.

Decisions that emphasize profit over fair working conditions or that fail to address the impact of globalization on domestic industries may, on the other hand, result in a widening of economic disparities. In the process of creating trade policy, political leaders are obligated to take into consideration the equilibrium that exists between economic growth and the welfare of workers.

Gaining Wealth and Having Access to Financial Services Political actions that pertain to financial rules and the availability of financial services are additional factors that contribute to the existence of income disparities. Individuals can be empowered to amass wealth and participate in economic activities through the implementation of policies that promote financial inclusion and access to credit. On the other hand, choices that prioritize the protection of financial institutions over consumer safeguards may be a factor in the accumulation of wealth and the growth of economic inequality.

One example of a political choice that can have a favorable impact on the distribution of income is the implementation of responsible lending practices, the promotion of financial literacy, and the guaranteeing of inexpensive banking services. Policymakers have the responsibility of navigating the regulatory landscape in order to cultivate a financial system that is inclusive and supports the equitable accumulation of wealth.

Considerations & Obstacles to Overcome:

In order to address the issue of income inequality, it is necessary to have political will and lobbying influence. The impact of large interest groups and lobbying efforts presents a hurdle. It is difficult to execute policies that prioritize social justice over the interests of affluent individuals or companies because political decisions can be influenced by entrenched interests. This makes it difficult to implement policies that promote social fairness.

Short-Term versus Long-Term aims: Political decisions are frequently impacted by electoral cycles, which results in a concentration on short-term aims that are more important than long-term objectives. In order to address income disparity, it is necessary to make efforts that are both long-term and sustainable. Policymakers may encounter difficulties when attempting to implement measures that produce outcomes that extend beyond the immediate political horizon.

In an interconnected global economy, political decisions in one country can be influenced by global economic dynamics. This is because global economic dynamics are affected by global economic dynamics. It is necessary to make a concerted effort on a global scale since many factors, such as trade ties, capital flows, and international economic conditions, might hinder the effectiveness of measures that are designed to reduce income disparity.

Displacement of Workers and technical breakthroughs The rapid speed of technical breakthroughs raises obstacles in the effort to reduce economic inequality. It is possible that automation and artificial intelligence will result in job displacement in specific areas. In order to ensure that persons who are impacted by this phenomenon have the opportunity to reskill and find employment in developing industries, it is necessary to implement regulations that are flexible.

A Way Forward for Addressing the Issue of Income Inequality

Implementation of Comprehensive Tax Reform: The implementation of comprehensive tax reform that ensures progressive tax rates, closes loopholes, and handles tax evasion can lead to a more fair distribution of wealth. It is imperative that policymakers give priority to tax measures that alleviate the burden placed on persons with low incomes while also ensuring that the wealthiest individuals contribute their fair amount.

Investment in Education: The decisions that are made by political leaders should give a high priority to making considerable investments in education at all levels. Among these are the elimination of inequalities in elementary, middle, and high school education, the reduction of the cost of higher education, and the provision of possibilities for vocational training. Policymakers have the ability to empower individuals to escape the cycle of poverty and contribute to economic progress by improving the accessibility and quality of high-quality educational opportunities.

Reforms in the Labor Market Political leaders should work toward labor market reforms that put workers' rights, workers' pay, and job security at the forefront of their priorities. A more inclusive labor market can be achieved by the implementation of policies that encourage collective bargaining, provide protections in the workplace, and strive to eliminate wage inequities. In addition, enhancing the adaptability of the workforce can be accomplished by providing support for projects that promote continual skill development and lifelong learning.

Programs of Social Welfare It is vital to maintain and strengthen social welfare programs in order to prevent the negative effects of income disparity. If policymakers want to enhance access to healthcare, affordable housing, and unemployment assistance, they should explore expanding these provision areas. Programs that are specifically designed to meet the requirements of underserved areas have the potential to make a contribution to the alleviation of poverty and the enhancement of the general well-being of society.

Global Cooperation on Trade: When it comes to trade policies, political decisions should give priority to trading practices that are both ethical and fair on a global scale. In order to build standards that guarantee workers' rights, environmental sustainability, and fair competition, policymakers ought to participate in international partnerships toward the establishment of these standards. Through the promotion of global economic policies that place a priority on social fairness, nations have the opportunity to collaborate in order to reduce income disparity on a comprehensive scale.

It is a complicated challenge that requires policymakers to undertake efforts that are both intelligent and sustained in order to address the impact of political and economic forces on income disparity. It is necessary to take a comprehensive approach in order to address the issue of income disparity. This approach should take into consideration taxation policies, education, labor market changes, social welfare programs, and global economic practices. A society that is more just and inclusive can be created by political decisions that emphasize social equity over short-term interests. These decisions can also foster economic stability and social cohesiveness, which are both to the benefit of all members of society. As governments struggle to come to terms with the complexities of this issue, it is essential that policymaking be done in a collaborative and adaptable manner in order to create a future in which income disparity is reduced and opportunities for success are distributed more fairly across society.

5.2 Social and cultural repercussions of economic decline

The economic decline, which is characterized by a decrease in economic activity, an increase in unemployment, and financial instability, has far-reaching ramifications that go beyond the obvious financial implications. There is a close relationship between the social and cultural fabric of a society and the economic well-being of that society. The purpose of this research is to give insight on the challenges, transformations, and potential pathways for resilience in the face of such hardship. The analysis investigates the substantial effects that economic decline has on social structures and cultural dynamics.

As a result of the economic downturn, there has been a noticeable and immediate increase in the number of people who are unemployed, which has led to social discontentment. Loss of employment increases the likelihood of individuals and families experiencing financial instability, which in turn contributes to increased levels of stress, anxiety, and a feeling of hopelessness. It is common for widespread unemployment to be accompanied with social unrest, which in turn helps to cultivate an atmosphere of frustration and disgust with established institutions.

In the same way that individuals struggle to cope with the difficulties of unemployment, social relationships may become strained as a result of the burden of financial distress, and groups may experience increased levels of tension simultaneously. An increase in the number of incidents of social unrest and discontentment can be attributed to the deterioration of job security, which can weaken the sense of stability that is the foundation of social harmony.

Influence on Mental Health and Well-Being The downturn in the economy has a substantial influence on both the mental health and well-being of individuals. An increase in the number of people experiencing mental health problems within a society can be attributed to the pressures that are connected with financial uncertainty, unemployment, and the fear of an unknown future. It is possible for individuals to suffer increased levels of anxiety, sadness, and other mental health issues while they navigate the economic slump.

There has been a general reduction in the mental well-being of the community as a whole, as well as an increase in the number of occurrences of domestic violence. These social ramifications of this mental health strain are obvious in the strained family relationships. In times of economic collapse, it is absolutely necessary to have a mental health support system that is resilient in order to mitigate the wide-ranging consequences for society.

Alterations in Consumption Patterns and Lifestyle Choices: When a society's economy is in a state of decline, it frequently causes a change in the consumption patterns and lifestyle choices that people make. It is possible that individuals and families will reduce their spending on discretionary items, which will result in a decrease in demand for goods and services that are not essential. This change will have repercussions for a variety of businesses, including employment possibilities and economic sectors that are dependent on consumer spending.

When it comes to culture, the calibration of consumption habits has the potential to change the norms and values of society. It is possible that the focus may move from material pursuits to more vital demands, which will lead to a reevaluation of the objectives that make up society. The cultural repercussions extend to the creative sectors, where changes in consumer behavior may have an impact on artistic expression, entertainment, and the manufacturing of cultural goods.

The impact of a declining economy on education and the development of skills is that it can cause disruptions in educational systems, which in turn restricts access to chances for skill development and excellent education. When there are financial limits, it is possible that educational institutions may receive less money, which will have an effect on the quality of education and restrict the resources available for programs that increase skills. It is possible that this could contribute to a widening skills gap, which would in turn exacerbate unemployment and impede the advancement of society.

A decrease in the number of educational possibilities available might result in a cultural shift toward a lessening of the importance placed on intellectual pursuits and creative undertakings. There is a possibility that a lack of access to quality education could inhibit the growth of a competent workforce, which in turn would limit the ability of a society to innovate and adapt to shifting economic landscapes.

Alterations in Cultural Values and Priorities: Downturns in the economy have the potential to bring about changes in the cultural values and priorities of society. It is possible for individuals and communities to reconsider their beliefs during times of financial adversity, placing a greater emphasis on resiliency, mutual support, and resourcefulness.

These shifting ideals may be reflected in cultural expressions such as art, literature, and the media, which can provide insights into the collective psychology of a society that is navigating the challenges of the economy.

On the other hand, a fall in the economy can also give rise to cultural tensions, as individuals and groups struggle to find a balance between conflicting goals. The larger cultural upheavals that are taking place as a result of the economic issues that are being faced are exemplified by the debates that take place over the distribution of resources, social support networks, and government action.

A deterioration in the economy can have a negative impact on social mobility and equality by exacerbating pre-existing social inequalities and making it more difficult for people to move. Existing inequalities can be exacerbated by factors such as restricted access to education, fewer job possibilities, and a lack of opportunities for economic advancement, which can result in a society that is more stratified. This has the potential to have significant repercussions on the social fabric, which can in turn generate a sense of injustice and resentment among communities who are disenfranchised.

It is possible that the story of social mobility and the promise of a better future may be subjected to criticism from a cultural perspective. An increase in social mobility poses a challenge to the fundamental principles that underpin the narrative of society, which in turn prompts a reassessment of the cultural norms and values that are associated with opportunities, success, and fairness.

Disintegration of Social Trust and Institutions The deterioration of the economy has the potential to destroy social trust and faith in institutions. It is possible that individuals' faith in the government, financial institutions, and society structures will decrease as they struggle to cope with the economic uncertainty they face. It can be difficult for communities to weather economic challenges collectively when there is a breakdown in social cohesion, which can be caused by skepticism and disillusionment with established structures.

The prevalent feeling of a society during periods of economic downturn is frequently reflected in the cultural expressions of that culture, such as art and literature. As a result of artists and producers reflecting the issues that their communities are experiencing, it is possible that themes of disillusionment, distrust, and social unrest will arise.

Impact on Family Structures and Dynamics A fall in the economy can put a significant amount of strain on the structures and dynamics of families.

There is a possibility that households will experience higher stress as a result of job losses, financial instability, and the requirement to implement additional austerity measures. It is possible for disruptions to occur in the typical roles and responsibilities of families, which can have an effect on the relationships that exist between spouses, parents, and children.

There is a possibility that cultural norms concerning the support of families and the relationships between generations would change as a result of economic difficulties. As households handle the intricacies of economic decline, there is a possibility that societal expectations surrounding the duties of family members will undergo a transition.

The Importance of Building Resilience and Mitigating Repercussions:

Investment in Social Safety Nets In order to address the social ramifications that are associated with a collapse in the economy, authorities should make the construction and maintenance of strong social safety nets a priority within their agenda. Individuals and families that are experiencing financial difficulties may benefit from comprehensive social welfare programs that include unemployment benefits, access to healthcare, and housing support. These programs can serve as a supporting mechanism.

A deliberate effort should be made to promote mental health support services in light of the fact that the influence of the economic downturn on mental health is something that should be taken into consideration. The broader societal effects that are connected with mental health difficulties can be mitigated via the investment in mental health infrastructure, counseling services, and community support networks.

Prioritizing Accessible Education and Skill Development In order to mitigate the impact on education and the development of skills, policymakers need to give priority to receiving an education that is both accessible and of high quality. Building a workforce that is more resilient and flexible can be accomplished through the implementation of programs that improve educational opportunities, reskilling programs, and vocational training for communities that are not traditionally served.

Fostering Inclusive Economic Policies In order to successfully navigate the current economic downturn, authorities should place a primary emphasis on the development of inclusive economic policies that tackle social inequalities. It is possible to contribute to the reduction of societal inequities through the implementation of progressive taxes, job development programs, and measures that prioritize equitable access to economic opportunities.

The arts, the media, and literature are all examples of cultural institutions that play an important part in reflecting and influencing societal narratives. Therefore, cultural initiatives for resilience are extremely important. During periods of economic downturn, cultural efforts that encourage resiliency, promote social cohesiveness, and address cultural issues can make a positive contribution to the general well-being of a society.

Developing community participation and support networks is vital for reducing the social implications of economic decline. This is because these networks are essential for fostering community engagement. Initiatives at the grassroots level, community-based organizations, and local support networks all play a part in the development of a sense of belonging and collective resilience within communities.

Individuals, families, and communities are all profoundly impacted by the social and cultural implications of economic decline, which are substantial and diverse in nature. Not only is it essential for individuals, but also for legislators and community leaders, to have a solid understanding of these repercussions. Through the implementation of preventative measures, the cultivation of resilience, and the prioritization of social well-being, societies are able to negotiate the obstacles that are posed by economic decline and strive toward the construction of a future that is more inclusive, flexible, and culturally vibrant.

Chapter 6

Industry-Specific Challenges

The economic landscape of the world is a dynamic tapestry that is woven with a variety of industries, each of which is confronted with difficulties that are distinct and molded by a myriad of circumstances. The combination of innovations in technology, regulatory settings, the dynamics of the market, and shocks from the outside world all contribute to the emergence of industry-specific difficulties. Within the scope of this investigation, the complexity of a number of important industries are investigated, along with the specific issues that these businesses face and the tactics that are utilized to navigate these complexities.

Manufacturing Industry: The manufacturing sector, which is a cornerstone of economic development, is confronted with a variety of issues in the current period. While automation and other modern technologies do improve efficiency, they also increase the likelihood of job displacement and necessitate the presence of a skilled labor force. In addition, disruptions in global supply chains, such as those that occurred during the COVID-19 epidemic, reveal vulnerabilities in manufacturing networks.

A major issue is the sustainability of the environment, and there is pressure to adopt practices that are beneficial to the environment. This requires industrial companies to make investments in environmentally friendly technologies and to conform to severe environmental standards, both of which can put a strain on the financial resources available to those businesses.

Embracing the technologies of Industry 4.0 for smart manufacturing, investing in workforce training programs, and diversifying supply chains to boost resilience are some of the strategies that must be implemented in order to successfully navigate these obstacles. It is absolutely necessary for countries, businesses, and environmental organizations to work together in order to develop and put into reality environmentally responsible policies and procedures.

Technology and the Information Technology Sector: The fast development of technology and the information technology sector has been accompanied by both opportunities and challenges. There are a number of obstacles that must be overcome in order to keep market relevance, including short product life cycles, fierce competition, and the ongoing requirement for innovation. There is a continual concern regarding cybersecurity, which necessitates large investments in order to protect sensitive information and keep the trust of consumers.

The process of navigating regulatory environments presents a difficulty for global technology companies, particularly when considering the context of data protection and digital governance considerations. When trying to find a balance between the pursuit of innovation and compliance with regulations, it becomes a delicate equilibrium to achieve.

Continuous investments in research and development, efforts to protect against cyberattacks, and participation in public-private partnerships to build regulatory frameworks are all strategies that are being implemented. When working in a field where change is not just constant but also exponential, adaptability and agility are essential skills to possess.

Healthcare and Pharmaceutical Industry: The healthcare and pharmaceutical industry is facing a number of distinct difficulties that are being driven by demographic trends, technological developments, and the complexities of regulatory frameworks. Populations that are getting older in many parts of the world are driving up the demand for healthcare, which necessitates the development of new solutions to alleviate the strain on healthcare systems.

Timelines for the development of new drugs, clearances from regulatory agencies, and the ever-increasing expense of research and development are all issues that the pharmaceutical business must contend with. Issues pertaining to intellectual property, such as the proliferation of generic competition and the expiration of patents, provide challenges to various revenue streams.

Among the strategies are the utilization of data analytics for the purpose of drug discovery, the promotion of relationships with research institutions, and the management of intricate regulatory procedures. It is essential to take patient-centered methods, precision medicine, and investments in digital health technologies into consideration in order to handle the changing landscape of the healthcare industry.

Energy & Renewable Resources: The energy sector is currently undergoing a fundamental shift, and it is struggling with the simultaneous difficulties of meeting the growing demand for energy on a worldwide scale while also transitioning towards sustainability. As a result of environmental concerns, conventional energy sources, such as fossil fuels, are being scrutinized, which leads to the necessity of transitioning towards alternatives that are renewable and cleaner.

Intermittent power, storage, and grid integration are all problems that the renewable energy business must contend with.

Additionally, the adoption and expansion of renewable technologies are impacted by economic factors, laws implemented by the government, and the perceptions of the general population.

Diversifying energy portfolios, getting investments in energy storage systems, and campaigning for regulations that are favorable are all strategies that can be implemented. In order to lead the energy sector toward a more sustainable future, public-private partnerships, international cooperation, and technological breakthroughs that are more energy efficient all play an important role.

Agriculture and Food sector: The agriculture and food sector faces a variety of issues, including the effects of climate change on crop yields, disruptions in supply chains, and shifting preferences among consumers. The concern for the environment, the lack of available water, and the requirement for environmentally responsible agricultural operations all add levels of complexity to the economy.

Farmers and food producers are exposed to potential dangers as a result of market volatility, which is impacted by a variety of factors including meteorological disasters and geopolitical conflicts. Additionally, the globalization of the food supply chain leads to the introduction of difficulties concerning the safety of food and the ability to trace it.

Some of the strategies that can be implemented are the utilization of technologies for precision agriculture, the diversity of crop types, and the implementation of sustainable agricultural methods. It is absolutely necessary for all parties involved in the food supply chain, from farmers to retailers, to work together in order to combat the difficulties that are associated with food security and sustainability.

Financial Services and Banking: The financial services industry operates in a dynamic environment that is formed by financial fluctuations, changes in regulatory policies, and disruptions brought about by technological advancements. Threats to cybersecurity, breaches of data security, and the requirement for comprehensive risk management are continuously occurring concerns. A large amount of resources and the flexibility to adapt are required in order to achieve regulatory compliance, particularly in the setting of constantly changing financial regulations.

It is important to note that technological improvements, such as the proliferation of fintech and digital currencies, bring about simultaneous opportunities and challenges.

The traditional financial institutions have to manage the shifting terrain in order to maintain their competitive edge while also addressing concerns over the safety of consumer data and the trust of their customers.

To implement strategies, it is necessary to embrace digital transformation, make investments in cybersecurity measures, and work together with innovators in the fintech industry. In an environment that is defined by rapid technological breakthroughs, it is vital for financial institutions to have the ability to adapt and to take an approach that is tailored to the needs of their customers.

Transportation and Logistics: The transportation and logistics industry is confronted with issues that are a result of globalization, disruptions caused by technological advancements, and concerns over sustainability. The need of constructing logistics networks that are both resilient and adaptable is brought into sharper focus by the interruptions that occurred in the supply chain during the COVID-19 epidemic.

There is an increasing emphasis on environmental sustainability, with pressure being put on to minimize carbon emissions and adopt transportation options that are beneficial to the environment. Traditional transportation and logistics companies are presented with opportunities as well as challenges as a result of the integration of autonomous cars and the expansion of e-commerce.

One strategy involves making investments in technology for the purpose of optimizing routes, finding solutions for last-mile deliveries, and implementing sustainability efforts such as electric cars. When it comes to addressing difficulties and influencing the future of transportation and logistics, collaboration between industry players, governments, and technology suppliers is absolutely necessary.

The intricate interaction of economic, technological, and regulatory issues is reflected in the various and ever-changing nature of the challenges that are peculiar to every industry. In order to successfully navigate these hurdles, a combination of creative thinking, adaptation, and strategic teamwork could be required. Industries that are able to successfully address the issues that are specific to them frequently act as catalysts for economic growth, technical improvement, and societal progress and development.

It is imperative that industries continue to maintain vigilance, proactivity, and resilience in the face of new difficulties as the global economic landscape continues to undergo transformation.

In order to cultivate an atmosphere that promotes innovation, sustainable practices, and equitable growth across a wide range of industries, policymakers, businesses, and other stakeholders need to work together. Building a solid basis for economic development and successfully navigating the complexity of the current industrial landscape are both possible for civilizations that take this course of action.

6.1 Examination of sectors facing the brunt of economic decline

The economic downturn, which is defined by a decrease in economic activity, an increase in unemployment, and financial instability, frequently shows itself in a manner that is not uniform throughout the various sectors. Certain sectors are especially susceptible to the difficulties that are brought about by economic downturns, and they are more likely to experience the negative effects of the economic decline than other sectors. In this examination, important sectors that carry the weight of economic concerns are investigated, and special attention is paid to the unique obstacles that these sectors face as well as the techniques that are utilized to navigate these difficulties.

One of the industries that is most vulnerable to a downturn in economic activity is the hospitality and tourism industry. It is common for consumers to cut their expenditure on non-essential services, such as travel and leisure activities, while the economy is in a slump. Hotels, restaurants, airlines, cruise lines, and other services, as well as other associated businesses, are all affected by the impact.

Consumers have a tendency to reduce their discretionary spending during times of economic instability, and vacation plans are frequently among the first things that are postponed or canceled as a result. This has a domino effect on businesses operating within the hotel and tourism industry, resulting in decreased occupancy rates, customers canceling their reservations, and in some instances, businesses closing their doors.

Increasing the variety of services offered, launching creative marketing initiatives, and forming collaborations with travel agencies are all strategies that can be utilized to strengthen resilience in this industry. There is also the possibility that firms will go to the government for assistance

and stimulus packages in order to weather the current economic troubles.

Retail and Consumer Goods: The retail and consumer goods sector is extremely vulnerable to variations in the economy since the spending patterns of consumers closely mirror the health of the economy. Consumers have a tendency to tighten their budgets during times of an economic downturn, hence limiting their discretionary expenditure on non-essential products. This has an effect on retailers, both those who operate online and those who operate traditional stores, as well as manufacturers and suppliers of consumer goods.

A decrease in sales for merchants is a result of a number of factors, including a loss in consumer confidence and a reduction in spending power. In a market that is uncertain, inventory management becomes an extremely important concern for firms as they attempt to strike a balance between supply and demand.

Resilience strategies in the retail industry include the implementation of e-commerce, the implementation of cost-cutting measures, and the adoption of an agile approach to inventory management. Other strategies that can be utilized to sustain client involvement during difficult economic times include the provision of discounts, promotions, and loyalty programs respectively.

As the economy continues to deteriorate, the automotive industry is confronted with a number of specific issues, which are frequently associated with a reduction in the demand from customers for expensive things. The purchase of an automobile is a big financial commitment; therefore, individuals may choose to postpone or forego such purchases when the economy is uncertain.

Automobile manufacturers, suppliers, and dealerships all experience decreased sales, production cuts, and the possibility of layoffs as a consequence of this. The susceptibility of the industry to economic collapse is worsened by a number of variables, including growing material costs, interruptions in global supply chains, and shifting preferences among consumers.

The diversification of vehicles into electric and hybrid vehicles, the implementation of cost-efficiency measures, and the formation of strategic alliances are all strategies for resilience. There is also the possibility that the industry could profit from government incentives for environmentally responsible and forward-thinking methods.

Real Estate and Construction: The real estate and construction industries are inextricably connected to economic cycles, and a fall in the economy has an effect on both the residential and commercial markets. It is common for a reduction in consumer confidence to result in a decrease in demand for real estate, which in turn has an impact on both property prices and sales volumes.

Due to the tightening of credit markets and the diminished interest of investors, construction projects, including residential and commercial developments, may experience delays or cancellations. When it comes to acquiring finance for projects, satisfying debt commitments, and handling unsold inventories, the industry contends with a number of obstacles.

The establishment of affordable housing, the investigation of public-private partnerships, and the diversification into property management and leasing services are all strategies that can be utilized to achieve resilience. In addition, adapting to shifting consumer tastes, such as the demand for environmentally friendly and technologically advanced homes, can be a factor in ensuring long-term profitability.

With the need for energy being strongly tied to economic activity, the oil and energy sector is especially susceptible to economic collapse. This is because the oil and energy sector involves the production of energy. When the economy is in a downturn, there is a reduction in the amount of energy that is consumed as a result of decreased industrial production and travel. The sector is also influenced by geopolitical events, supply gluts, and volatility in oil prices, among other variables.

The profitability of exploration and production businesses is negatively impacted by low oil prices, which in turn leads to a reduction in investments related to new projects. At the same time that it presents traditional oil and gas corporations with opportunity, the transition toward renewable energy sources also presents them with obstacles.

The diversification of energy sources into renewable sources, the implementation of cost-cutting measures, and the formation of strategic alliances are all strategies for resilience. It is also possible for businesses operating in this industry to investigate ways to improve the efficiency of their extraction and production processes in order to sustain their profitability during times of economic downturn.

Financial Services and Banking: Despite the fact that financial services and banking are vital components of the economy, they are not immune to the difficulties that come with an economic downturn. In addition to increased loan defaults, decreased consumer expenditure, and volatile market conditions, the industry is also exposed to dangers like these.

As consumers and businesses become more risk-averse, there is a possibility that banks will see a decrease in the amount of money they lend out. Additionally, financial institutions are confronted with the challenge of adjusting to shifting regulatory frameworks and the influence that low interest rates have on their businesses' profitability.

The implementation of smart risk management, cost-efficiency measures, and diversification of service offerings are all strategies that contribute to resilience.

In order for financial institutions to effectively manage the problems that the economy presents, it is essential for them to collaborate with fintech innovators, undergo digital transformation, and implement a customer-centric approach.

Certain industries are particularly vulnerable to the effects of economic downturns because of their susceptibility to changes in consumer spending habits, market demand, and external factors such as the prices of commodities and the state of the world economy. The tourist and hospitality industry, retail and consumer goods, the automobile industry, real estate and construction, the oil and energy industry, and the banking and financial services industry are among the industries that are most susceptible to swings in the economy.

Utilizing a combination of strategic planning, innovation, and adaptability is necessary in order to achieve resilience in these industries. The diversification of services, the use of cost-cutting measures, the investment in technology, and the engagement with stakeholders are all prevalent tactics that are utilized by firms operating within areas that are vulnerable. It is the responsibility of policymakers to provide businesses with the necessary support, stimulus packages, and regulatory frameworks that will allow them to successfully traverse the problems that the economy presents.

In order to successfully negotiate the difficulties of economic decline, businesses operating in these industries need to maintain vigilance, agility, and a proactive attitude as the global economy continues to undergo change. It is possible for firms to position themselves to weather economic problems and contribute to the overall economic recovery if they embrace innovation, sustainability, and strategic alliances.

6.2 Implications for innovation and technological advancement

The panorama of innovation and technological advancement is heavily impacted by economic challenges, which are characterized by downturns, uncertainty, and disruptions. Despite the fact that economic troubles might hinder the availability of resources and investments, they can serve as a driving force behind the development of innovative solutions and revolutionary changes. The purpose of this research is to investigate the effects that economic difficulties have on technological advancement and innovation. Specifically, the analysis will investigate the opportunities and restrictions that arise in contexts that are so dynamic.

Constraints on Research and Development (R&D) expenditure Constrained budgets and decreased expenditure across a variety of industries, including research and development (R&D), are frequently the result of economic difficulties. The allocation of resources to innovative ventures may be difficult for businesses of all sizes, including those that are quite tiny.

It is possible that this restriction on spending on research and development may slow down the development of innovative solutions and prevent the advancement of ground-breaking innovations.

When faced with such circumstances, firms are required to prioritize their research and development activities, concentrating on projects that have the most potential for impact and profits. Despite the fact that this limitation may slow down the rate of innovation, it also encourages firms to streamline their research endeavors, which in turn fosters an approach that is more focused and strategic.

Impact on New Businesses and Small Businesses: New businesses and small businesses, which are frequently at the forefront of technological innovation, are more susceptible to the effects of economic difficulties. The expansion and continued existence of these businesses may be hampered by factors such as difficulty in gaining access to money, a decline in investor confidence, and a harsh economic environment.

On the other hand, economic downturns can also stimulate creative thinking among entrepreneurs. There is a possibility that startups will be motivated to discover solutions that are more cost-effective, to utilize lean approaches, and to investigate creative business models. The challenges that are encountered by entrepreneurs have the potential to cultivate a culture of resiliency, adaptability, and resourcefulness, which will ultimately end up leading to an entrepreneurial ecosystem that is more robust and agile.

Changes in Innovation Priorities: When the economy is in a difficult state, there is frequently a change in the priorities that govern innovation. It is possible for companies to shift their attention to technologies that improve efficiency, lower costs, and provide solutions to pressing problems. It is possible that this will result in a greater focus being placed on inventions that provide measurable and rapid returns on investment.

Although there is a possibility that initiatives that are both revolutionary and long-term could experience delays, the reorientation of innovation goals may result in the development of solutions that are both practical and fulfill the urgent demands of businesses and consumers. As a result of this adaptability to changing conditions, the dynamic nature of innovation is highlighted during times of economic difficulty.

Increased Collaboration and Open Innovation: When the economy is in a tough position, collaboration becomes an essential strategy for innovation.

Research projects that involve collaboration between businesses, the sharing of resources, and the formation of partnerships to pool expertise are all possibilities. Open innovation, which is a form of collaboration between businesses and entities from the outside world, is becoming increasingly popular as a means of gaining access to extra resources, expertise, and viewpoints.

Not only does the collaborative approach make it possible for firms to share the risks and costs associated with innovation, but it also quickens the rate at which technical advancements are making progress. When industry firms, academic institutions, and government agencies work together to form partnerships, they have the potential to generate synergies that can lead to breakthroughs, even when the economic conditions are difficult.

Intervention by the government and the provision of incentives for innovation: When the economy is in a state of crisis, governments frequently play a vital role in determining the landscape of innovation. A number of methods, including research grants, tax incentives, and stimulus packages, are frequently utilized by governments in order to foster innovation. By providing financial assistance to research and development operations, governments hope to hasten the development of new technologies and to boost economic expansion.

In addition, the engagement of the government may involve the development of innovation hubs, incubators, and accelerators in order to provide assistance to new businesses and other small businesses. The implementation of these activities results in the formation of an ecosystem that encourages collaboration, the sharing of knowledge, and the creation of new solutions across a variety of industries.

The importance of digital transformation is emphasized since economic difficulties frequently hasten the adoption of digital technology by firms. These businesses are looking to streamline their operations, strengthen their resilience, and investigate new revenue streams. Organizations are increasing their investments in technology such as artificial intelligence, cloud computing, and data analytics as the demand for digital transformation grows more intense.

Despite the fact that the initial expenses associated with digital transformation may present a barrier, the long-term benefits, which include enhanced efficiency, agility, and competitiveness, can put firms in a position to achieve continuous success. The economic challenges that companies face serve as a catalyst for them to adopt technologies that boost their digital capabilities and their responsiveness to the dynamics of the market.

Pay Attention to Sustainability and Resilience: While the economy is experiencing difficulties, sustainability and resilience become important factors to take into consideration while developing innovation initiatives. Companies are becoming more aware of the significance of technologies that not only help to the expansion of the economy but also to the preservation of the environment and the improvement of the well-being of society. The increasing alignment of firms' strategies with long-term sustainability goals has led to an increase in the popularity of innovations in areas such as sustainable agriculture, circular economies, and renewable energy.

The emphasis placed on resilience extends beyond environmental concerns to include the resilience of supply chains, the continuity of economic operations, and the management of various crises. When it comes to navigating economic uncertainty, technological innovations that promote resilience, such as comprehensive data analytics for risk assessment, are becoming increasingly important.

Opportunities for Disruptive Innovation: Economic difficulties provide a fertile environment for disruptive innovation, which may be defined as the advancement of technology or business models that bring about a significant transformation in various industries. Disruptions can be caused by a number of factors, including the desire for cost efficiency, shifting consumer behaviors, or a reevaluation of old company methods.

During times of economic instability, organizations that are innovative and entrepreneurial may be able to find holes in the market and provide solutions that question the conventions that are currently in place. These inventions have the ability to restructure industries, generate new markets, and drive economic recovery. They also have the capacity to create innovation.

The processes of innovation and technological advancement are dynamic processes that are a response to the challenges and opportunities that are given by economic downturns. Constraints on resources and expenditure on research and development present problems; yet, they also help to cultivate a culture that prioritizes efficiency and strategic focus. Even if they are fragile, startups and small businesses exhibit resilience and innovation, which contributes to an environment that is more agile for entrepreneurs.

Innovation priorities have shifted, collaboration has increased, and government engagement has expanded, all of which create opportunities for breakthroughs even in the face of adverse economic conditions. The digital transition, issues of sustainability, and disruptive technologies are emerging as significant themes that will shape the future trajectory of technological growth.

The consequences for innovation and technological advancement during times of economic difficulty underscore the adaptable nature of organizations as well as the transformative potential of forces that are disruptive. The ability to strategically exploit innovation becomes an increasingly important factor in determining long-term success and resilience on the part of companies as they navigate the economic uncertainties that they face.

Chapter 7

Potential Solutions

An all-encompassing strategy is required in order to alleviate the effects of economic obstacles and to encourage recovery, regardless of whether these issues are the result of global crises, recessions, or unexpected disruptions. There are various yet interwoven roles that individuals, businesses, and governments play in the process of addressing economic challenges inside the economy. In this analysis, viable solutions across all of these sectors are investigated, with a particular emphasis placed on measures that have the potential to contribute to resilience, adaptation, and sustained economic well-being.

Individuals' Solutions to the Problem:

Planning and Financial Literacy: Individuals can improve their ability to withstand the effects of economic challenges by making an investment in their economic planning and financial literacy. An individual's ability to weather financial uncertainty is directly correlated to their level of knowledge regarding personal finance, budgeting, and wise investing techniques. At both the individual and the community level, the promotion of financial literacy can be significantly aided by educational efforts, workshops, and resources that are easily accessible.

Skill improvement and Lifelong Learning: Individuals are required to demonstrate adaptability and continual skill improvement in order to keep up with the quickly changing economic landscape. It is possible to improve one's employability and career resilience by making investments in education and obtaining new skills. It is possible for governments and businesses to make a contribution by making available training programs, offering online courses, and giving possibilities for vocational training that are in accordance with the requirements of new industries.

It is important for individuals to diversify their income streams because relying on a single source of income can leave them susceptible to the effects of economic shocks. Increasing the number of sources of income that you have, such as by engaging in freelance work, starting a side business, or participating in the gig economy, can provide you with more financial security. Support for this can be provided by governments through the creation of an environment that is conducive to entrepreneurship, the simplification of regulatory procedures, and the provision of incentives for initiatives involving small businesses.

Building Up Your Emergency Savings: One of the most important strategies that individuals may employ in order to navigate the economic uncertainties that they face is to keep a substantial emergency savings reserve. Promoting a culture of financial preparation can be accomplished by encouraging people to develop the habit of saving money through the use of tax incentives, employer-sponsored savings programs, and financial literacy campaigns.

Having access to affordable healthcare is important since the costs of medical care can be a considerable burden amid adverse economic conditions. It is possible to contribute to the overall well-being of individuals and reduce the financial pressure that is associated with medical emergencies by ensuring that persons have access to inexpensive healthcare through public health programs, insurance coverage, and preventative measures.

Solutions for Companies and Organizations:

Businesses can improve their resilience by adopting agile and flexible business models. This is one way that businesses can improve their resilience. This entails conducting regular reassessments of the dynamics of the market, the behaviors of consumers, and the trends in the sector in order to promptly adjust to changing conditions. The adoption of digital technology, the utilization of data analytics, and the cultivation of an innovative culture all contribute to the adaptiveness that is necessary to succeed in economic conditions that are fraught with uncertainty.

Supply Chain Diversification and Resilience: The importance of resilient and diverse supply chains is brought to light by the occurrence of global disruptions. Diversifying suppliers, investigating their alternatives for local sourcing, and putting in place effective risk management methods are all ways in which businesses can reduce their exposure to risk. The creation of incentives for supply chain resilience and the promotion of cooperation between industry actors are two measures that governments might take to help this endeavor.

Remote Work and Flexibility: The COVID-19 pandemic has hastened the acceptability of working from a remote location. It is possible for businesses to improve the resilience and continuity of their staff by adopting flexible work arrangements, which may include the opportunity to work remotely. It is possible for governments to provide assistance for this shift by making investments in digital infrastructure, advocating flexible labor legislation, and offering incentives to enterprises that implement policies that allow for remote employment.

Financial Planning and Contingency Funds: Good financial planning and the formation of contingency funds are essential for companies that are experiencing difficulties in the economy. The maintenance of sufficient liquidity, the responsible management of debt, and the accumulation of reserves all contribute to the stability of the financial system.

The provision of low-interest loans, grants, and other financial incentives to firms in order to assist them in retaining their liquidity is something that governments may easily facilitate.

In order for businesses to successfully navigate the economic uncertainties, it is essential for them to have customer-centric approaches that allow them to comprehend and react to the shifting behaviors of consumers. By adopting customer-centric techniques, such as individualized marketing strategies, proactive customer service, and creative product offerings, firms are able to maintain a competitive edge in industries that are always evolving.

Investment in Technology and Innovation: In order for organizations to maintain their competitive edge, it is critically important for them to make investments in technology and cultivate a culture of innovation. This can be supported by governments through the provision of subsidies for research and development, the establishment of innovation hubs, and the provision of incentives for the adoption of technology. Technologies that contribute to economic growth can be driven via collaboration between corporations and research institutes, which can also promote technical improvements.

Possible Solutions for Organizations:

Packages of Economic Stimulus: The implementation of targeted stimulus packages by governments is an essential component in minimizing the impact of economic problems. It is possible for these packages to contain direct cash assistance for individuals, businesses, and industries who are going through the most difficult times economically. When the economy is experiencing a crisis, the rapid deployment of stimulus measures can help infuse cash into the economy and prevent a prolonged recession.

Infrastructure Investment: Investing in infrastructure projects is a great way to boost economic activity, generate employment opportunities, and strengthen the economy's ability to withstand long-term challenges. It is possible for governments to allot cash to projects that aim to develop digital infrastructure, transportation, renewable energy, and healthcare facilities. These kinds of investments, in addition to contributing to the economic recovery, also establish the groundwork for continued growth.

Provision of Assistance to Small and Medium-Sized Businesses (SMEs): Small and medium-sized businesses are extremely important contributors to the growth of the economy. Small and medium-sized enterprises (SMEs) can receive targeted help from governments in the form of low-interest loans, grants, and programs that improve capacity. Both entrepreneurship and innovation are encouraged by the simplification of regulatory procedures, the reduction of bureaucratic obstacles, and the creation of an atmosphere that is beneficial to business.

Policies Regarding the Labor Market: Policies that are flexible in the labor market and that strike a balance between worker protection and business flexibility lead to a workforce that is resilient. Governments have the ability to modify labor legislation in order to accommodate shifting work dynamics, provide support for projects that aim to increase workers' skills, and encourage fair labor practices. Workers are provided with a safety net in the form of social safety nets, which include unemployment compensation and healthcare coverage, when the economy is experiencing difficulties.

Projects for Digital Transformation: Governments have the ability to drive digital transformation projects in order to position their economies for future success. Investments in digital infrastructure, encouragement of the use of digital technology in commercial enterprises, and the promotion of electronic governance are all necessary steps in this direction. Through the implementation of digital literacy programs, the workforce is provided with the skills necessary to participate in the digital economy.

Policies that are both sustainable and inclusive: Policies that are both sustainable and inclusive contribute to the long-term economic sustainability of a country. In order to address issues of wealth inequality, social inclusion, and environmental sustainability, governments have the ability to adopt legislation that encourages ecologically responsible behaviors. The aims of sustainable development can serve as a guide for policies, helping to guarantee that economic progress is in line with the well-being of society and the environment.

Collaboration on a Global Scale: In order to address global challenges, international cooperation is required. In order to encourage international collaboration on issues such as trade, climate change, and public health, governments have the ability to engage in diplomatic endeavors. Initiatives that include collaboration, such as joint research projects and agreements to share knowledge, contribute to the stability of the global economy and generate prospects for economic recovery.

An approach that is multidimensional and collaborative, engaging individuals, corporations, and governments, is required in order to address the issues that the economy is facing. Education, the development of skills, and sensible financial planning are all ways in which individuals might strengthen their ability to withstand financial hardship. The adoption of agile methods, the diversification of supply chains, and the investment in technology are all ways in which businesses can learn to navigate uncertainty. The provision of economic stimulation, the provision of support to enterprises, and the implementation of policies that enhance sustainability and inclusivity are all very important roles that governments play.

The interconnection of activities across these different sectors is brought to light by the potential solutions that have been presented. The combination of individual empowerment, the resilience of businesses, and the participation of the government results in the creation of a comprehensive framework for navigating the obstacles that the economy presents. It is possible that the proactive deployment of these solutions can help to sustain economic well-being and resilience as societies continue to adjust to changing economic landscapes.

7.1 Policy recommendations for economic revitalization

A complete collection of policies that aim to stimulate development, create innovation, and enhance resilience is required in order to implement economic revival, which is a difficult endeavor that requires such policies. As a result of the difficulties that the economy is experiencing, governments play a crucial part in the process of designing and putting into action policies that encourage recovery and sustainable development. The purpose of this analysis is to investigate major policy ideas across a variety of dimensions in order to direct efforts to revitalize the economy.

Recommendations Regarding Fiscal Policy:

Stimulus Packages of a Targeted Nature:

When the economy is in a downturn, one of the most important fiscal policy measures that may be implemented is tailored stimulus packages. The packages that are being proposed have to incorporate direct financial assistance for individuals, organizations, and industries that are most impacted by the economic issues. Facilitating the injection of cash into the economy through the rapid deployment of stimulus measures helps to prevent a prolonged recession.

An Investment in the Infrastructure:

The allocation of cash for infrastructure projects not only encourages economic activity but also causes the creation of jobs and builds the groundwork for growth over the long run. The investments that are made in digital infrastructure, transportation, renewable energy, and healthcare facilities not only contribute to the immediate recovery of the economy, but they also boost the overall competitiveness of the economy.

Budgeting that is flexible and the distribution of resources:

The implementation of flexible budgeting procedures enables governments to effectively reallocate resources in accordance with the shifting priorities of the population. During the process of economic revitalization, giving spending priority to essential areas such as education, healthcare, and technology helps to cultivate resilience and provides the workforce with the skills necessary for successful participation in the digital economy.

Policy Recommendations Regarding Monetary Policy:

Measures to Manage Interest Rates:

It is possible for central banks to efficiently manage interest rates by utilizing the tools of monetary policy. Encouragement of borrowing, stimulation of investments, and support for consumer spending can all be achieved through the maintenance of accommodating interest rates during the process of economic revival. In order to better manage market expectations, central banks should communicate their stance on interest rates in a clear and comprehensive manner.

An Overview of Asset Purchases and Quantitative Easing:

In order to pump liquidity into the financial markets, central banks have the ability to participate in operations such as quantitative easing and asset purchases. The long-term interest rates can be lowered as a result, lending can be encouraged, and asset prices can be supported. Increasing confidence in the financial markets can be accomplished through open and honest information regarding the duration and scope of such actions.

The Targeting of Inflation:

The adoption of a specific inflation target serves as a framework for the implementation of monetary policy. The ability to adjust interest rates with greater flexibility is made possible by a moderate inflation objective during the period of economic recovery. For the purpose of establishing a foundation for inflation expectations, central banks should explain their inflation targets and methods to the general public.

Policies that are Particular to Businesses and Industries:

Assistance to Small and Medium-Sized Businesses (often known as SMEs):

It is crucial for small and medium-sized enterprises (SMEs) to get targeted support in order to ensure their continued existence and growth. In order to assist small and medium-sized enterprises (SMEs) in navigating economic issues, governments might offer low-interest loans, subsidies, and programs that create capacity. Simplifying regulatory procedures and lowering the number of obstacles posed by bureaucracy are two ways to encourage innovation and entrepreneurship.

Initiatives with Regard to Digital Transformation:

The competitiveness of enterprises can be improved through the implementation of digital transformation programs that are driven by governments.

Investing in digital infrastructure, offering financial incentives to encourage the adoption of technology, and encouraging e-governance are all factors that contribute to the rejuvenation of the economy. Through the implementation of digital literacy programs, the workforce is provided with the skills necessary to participate in the digital economy.

An incentive program for research and development (R&D):

In order to sustain economic growth over the long term, it is essential to provide incentives for research and development. Businesses that are active in research and innovation may be eligible for tax credits, grants, and subsidies from their respective governments. Accelerating technical developments and contributing to economic recovery are both positive outcomes that can be achieved through collaboration between businesses and research institutes.

Labor Market and Social Policies:

Regulations of the Labor Market That Are Candid:

The regulations that govern the flexible labor market achieve a compromise between the protection of workers and the flexibility of businesses. Governments have the ability to modify labor legislation in order to accommodate shifting work dynamics, provide support for projects that aim to increase workers' skills, and encourage fair labor practices. Workers are provided with a safety net in the form of social safety nets, which include unemployment compensation and healthcare coverage, when the economy is experiencing difficulties.

Education and the Development of Competencies:

It is essential to make investments in education and the development of skills in order to construct a labor force that is capable of meeting the requirements of the modern economy. The provision of accessible training programs, online courses, and chances for vocational training should be a priority for governments, and they should invest resources accordingly. Initiatives on lifelong learning ensure that persons are able to adapt to the changing requirements of the industry.

The Policies Regarding the Environment and Sustainability:

Investments in Environmentally Friendly Infrastructure:

It is necessary to make investments in green infrastructure projects in order to align the efforts of economic regeneration with the goals of sustainability. It is possible for governments to allot cash for projects involving renewable energy, technology that are efficient with energy, and activities that promote sustainable mobility. Not only do these investments increase employment opportunities, but they also help to preserve the natural environment.

A Regulatory Structure for Environmental Sustainability:

Establishing a legislative framework that provides incentives for environmentally responsible practices is absolutely necessary. Businesses can be encouraged to embrace environmentally friendly practices, social inclusion can be promoted, and wealth disparity can be addressed through the implementation of legislation that governments can set. The aims of sustainable development can serve as a guide for policies, helping to guarantee that economic progress is in line with the well-being of society and the environment.

International Cooperation and Trade Policies:

Attempts at Diplomacy in the Interest of International Cooperation:

The resuscitation of the economy requires assistance from international partners. It is imperative that governments participate in diplomatic initiatives in order to encourage international collaboration on issues pertaining to public health, climate change, and trade. Initiatives that include collaboration, such as joint research projects and agreements to share knowledge, contribute to the stability of the global economy and generate prospects for economic recovery.

Promotion of Open Markets and Trade Facilitation:

The reduction of trade obstacles, the simplification of customs procedures, and the promotion of free markets are all ways in which governments can ease commerce. Through the diversification of revenue streams and the creation of possibilities for enterprises to pursue worldwide expansion, the promotion of international trade strengthens the economic resilience of a nation.

An approach that takes into account fiscal, monetary, industry-specific, labor market, social, environmental, and international policies is required in order to successfully revitalize the economy, which is a complex problem that requires a holistic approach. In order for these policies to be effective, it is necessary for government agencies, private companies, and international partners to work together in cooperation. Governments have the ability to create an environment that is conducive to sustainable growth, innovation, and resilience by adopting a comprehensive set of policies that address the various facets of economic difficulties. As nations traverse the intricacies of economic regeneration, policies that are purposeful and properly calibrated become increasingly important in laying the groundwork for a robust and adaptable economic future.

7.2 The role of public-private partnerships in recovery efforts

Partnerships between the public sector and the private sector, also known as PPPs, have developed as important vehicles for addressing economic difficulties and supporting development. In order to handle difficult issues, boost growth, and create resilience, the collaboration between public and private institutions brings together a wide variety of resources, experience, and capacities. Within the context of economic recovery efforts, this paper investigates the essential role that public-private partnerships (PPPs) play, analyzing their significance across a variety of industries and identifying critical success criteria.

The Acquisition of Basic Infrastructure:

Infrastructure development is one of the key sectors in which public-private partnerships (PPPs) play an important role in the economic recovery process. Governments frequently confront budgetary limits, which restrict their capacity to provide funding for projects of a significant magnitude. Participation from the private sector in the financing, designing, construction, and operation of infrastructure projects, such as transportation networks, energy facilities, and public utilities, is made possible through public-private partnerships (PPPs).

Projects including energy generation, public transit networks, and toll roads are all examples of successful public-private partnerships (PPPs) in the infrastructure sector. The acceleration of the delivery of essential infrastructure, the creation of jobs, and the stimulation of economic activity are all possible outcomes for governments that leverage private investment. PPPs, which are characterized by their risk-sharing structure, guarantee that both public and private players have a vested interest in the accomplishment of the project.

Innovation and the Implementation of New Technologies:

Through public-private partnerships (PPPs), innovative technology and practices can be more easily incorporated into public services and infrastructure. Partners from the private sector frequently bring cutting-edge skills and technologies to the table, which can improve the efficiency and efficacy of public projects being undertaken. The implementation of digital solutions, data analytics, and other technical improvements is made possible by public-private partnerships (PPPs) in industries such as healthcare, education, and smart cities.

In the context of a smart city program, for instance, a public-private partnership (PPP) could incorporate private enterprises that offer expertise in urban planning, Internet of Things (IoT) solutions, and data management. By incorporating innovation through public-private partnerships (PPPs), governments have the ability to update public services, establish a business environment that is more dynamic and competitive, and provide the economy with the foundation for continuous growth.

The creation of jobs and the stimulation of the economy:

The development of new jobs is an essential component during periods of economic rejuvenation. PPPs, particularly when it comes to projects involving infrastructure, have an effect that is direct on employment. Employing a diverse workforce is necessary for the development and operation of infrastructure, which results in the creation of jobs in the construction, maintenance, operations, and related service sectors.

In the case of the construction of a new airport, for instance, a public-private partnership (PPP) might result in the employment of construction workers, engineers, administrative personnel, and a variety of service providers. As a result of the multiplier impact of job creation, local economies are stimulated. This is because workers spend their earnings on goods and services, which contributes to a wider economic recovery.

Risk Management and the Effective Delivery of Projects:

Public-private partnerships (PPPs) provide a strategic avenue for risk control in complicated projects. A reduction in the possibility of project delays and cost overruns can be achieved by the sharing of risks between public and private parties. When private organizations are involved, they frequently contribute financial discipline, knowledge in project management, and operational efficiency, which ultimately results in the execution of projects that are more streamlined and on schedule.

While the private sector places a strong emphasis on cost-effectiveness and performance-based outcomes, governments reap the benefits of this approach. When public-private partnership (PPP) agreements are well-structured, risks such as construction delays, operational challenges, and variations in revenue are divided among the partners in accordance with their respective capabilities. This method of risk-sharing ensures that all parties are on the same page with regard to the successful completion of the project.

Financing and the Utilization of Available Resources:

Public-private partnerships (PPPs) provide a means by which governments can gain access to extra funds and resources without placing an excessive load on public budgets. Public-private partnerships (PPPs) are appealing to private investors and financiers because of the possibility for projects to generate money. Some examples of such projects are toll roads, utilities, and other infrastructure assets. This makes it possible for governments to pursue big initiatives that might be difficult to finance using traditional methods of public financing.

The private sector contributes specialized skills and knowledge, in addition to financial resources, when public-private partnerships (PPPs) are involved.

It is the responsibility of private partners, whether they be service providers, technology businesses, or construction companies, to contribute their knowledge in order to guarantee the prosperity of the project. The entire capabilities of the partnership are improved as a result of this engagement, which also helps to facilitate the transition of information between the public and private sectors.

Sustainability of the Environment:

PPPs have the potential to play a significant part in the attainment of environmental sustainability goals. Partners from the private sector frequently provide experience in areas such as environmentally responsible practices, renewable energy, and conservation of the environment. PPPs have the potential to incorporate environmentally friendly technologies and design ideas that are in line with environmental requirements into infrastructure projects.

For instance, a public-private partnership (PPP) in a renewable energy project can involve partnerships with private companies that specialize in wind or solar energy. Both the public and private sectors have the opportunity to make a contribution to the protection of the environment, as well as to the fulfillment of energy requirements and the promotion of economic growth, through the incorporation of sustainability into the project.

Participation in the Community and Its Influence on Society:

Partnerships that are successful give community participation a high priority and take into account the social impact of projects. Partners from the public sector and the business sector work together to ensure that projects are in line with the requirements and preferences of the community. The acceptance and support of initiatives within the local populace is increased through the utilization of this collaborative method.

Private construction companies, the local government, and community organizations could all be involved in a public-private partnership (PPP) project for the development of public housing, for instance. Including local stakeholders in project development helps to ensure that initiatives are sensitive to cultural norms, address issues raised by the community, and make a constructive contribution to the social fabric of the area.

Points of Success in Public-Private Partnerships:

A Clearly Defined Objective and a Responsibility:

For public-private partnerships (PPPs) to be successful, it is necessary to have specified objectives and accountability procedures.

Everyone involved in the project, whether public or private, ought to have a common knowledge of the project's objectives, timetables, and anticipated results.

Processes of Procurement That Are Both Open and Transparent:

When trying to attract qualified private partners, it is essential to have procurement processes that are both transparent and equitable. The use of open competition helps to ensure that the most suitable entities are chosen, which in turn ensures that efficiency is increased and corruption is avoided.

Assessment and Management of Risks That Are More Comprehensive:

It is necessary to be in possession of comprehensive risk assessment and management strategies. The resilience of the partnership can be improved by identifying possible risks and putting in place systems for risk sharing and mitigation.

Framework of Legal and Regulatory Concerns:

The necessary structure for public-private partnerships (PPPs) is provided by a distinct legislative and regulatory framework. Guidelines that are unambiguous about the enforcement of contracts, the resolution of disputes, and compliance with regulations all help to the stability of partnerships.

Contract Design That Allows for Flexibility:

PPPs are more likely to be successful when they have contract designs that are flexible and can be adapted to changing circumstances. A greater degree of adaptability is achieved by the partnership through the inclusion of provisions for renegotiation, performance-based rewards, and shared risk management measures.

Engagement of Stakeholders and Communication, Including:

Broad support for public-private partnerships (PPPs) can be ensured by effective communication with stakeholders, including the general public. Increasing the level of transparency, addressing concerns, and engaging local communities are all factors that contribute to the success of projects over the long run.

Partnerships between the public sector and the private sector are effective tools for economic recovery because they use the characteristics of both sectors to tackle difficult problems. Participatory public-private partnerships (PPPs) contribute to the resilience and dynamism of economies by encouraging innovation, the creation of jobs, the reduction of risks, and sustainable development.

To ensure the effectiveness of public-private partnerships (PPPs) in economic recovery efforts, collaborative efforts between governments, commercial entities, and communities are required. These efforts should place an emphasis on openness, accountability, and community participation. Leveraging the potential of public-private partnerships (PPPs) continues to be a strategic necessity for building equitable, sustainable, and resilient economic growth as societies continue to negotiate the complexities of economic difficulties.

Chapter 8

Future Outlook

The future is a landscape that is shaped by dynamic forces, where economic, technological, and social aspects converge to define the trajectory of human progress. This landscape is the future. In light of the fact that we are at the beginning of a period that will be marked by rapid change, uncertainty, and problems that have never been seen before, it is absolutely necessary to investigate the many different aspects of the future view. This analysis digs into the projected trends, problems, and opportunities that will contribute to the formation of the social, technological, and economic landscapes in the years to come.

Perspectives on the Economy:

In the aftermath of the pandemic:

It is anticipated that the ongoing effects of the COVID-19 pandemic would continue to have an effect on the economic landscape for the foreseeable future. In spite of the fact that broad immunization efforts have made it possible for communities to settle back into routine, the pandemic's scars are still visible. Dealing with broken supply networks, rethinking work patterns, and navigating the long-term effects of enormous fiscal stimuli are all necessary steps on the path to economic recovery.

Capacity for Resilience and Adaptation:

The outlook for the economy in the future places an emphasis on the significance of adaptability and resilience. Organizations and economies that are able to demonstrate the capacity to adapt, innovate, and remain resilient in the face of shocks will be in a better position to achieve success. The lessons that were learned from the epidemic highlight the importance of having diversified supply chains, a robust digital infrastructure, and contingency preparation.

Goals for Sustainable Development Include:

The global commitment to achieving sustainable development goals will have an impact on the policies and practices that govern the economy in the future. There is a growing awareness among governments, businesses, and investors regarding the significance of environmental, social, and governance (ESG) elements in the decision-making process. In order to achieve sustainable economic development, it will be essential to concentrate on the pursuit of a green economy, social inclusion, and ethical business practices.

The Transformation of Digital:

It is anticipated that the rapid pace of digital transformation that was observed during the epidemic will continue at its current pace. Artificial intelligence, the Internet of Things, and blockchain are examples of technologies that will continue to transform industries, increase productivity, and as well as develop new methods of business. Work, communication, and business will all undergo fundamental transformations as a result of the widespread adoption of digital technology across all industries. Those governments and enterprises who make investments in digital infrastructure and cultivate an innovative culture will be at the forefront of this revolution.

Dynamic aspects of globalization:

The trajectory of globalization is currently being reexamined during this time. When it comes to the global landscape, the interdependence of economies continues to be an essential component; yet, the dynamics of international trade and collaboration are undergoing significant change. It is possible for governments to reevaluate their trade policies, supply chain dependencies, and geopolitical considerations, which could result in a recalibrating of globalization initiatives.

Growth of the Economy Benefiting All:

There will be a strong emphasis placed on the pursuit of economic growth that is inclusive. In order to construct economies that are resilient and sustainable, it will be essential to address issues of income inequality, promote financial inclusion, and guarantee equal access to opportunities. It will be necessary for governments and corporations to develop policies that promote social mobility and contribute to the closing of socioeconomic gaps.

Alterations in the Labor Markets:

Transformations of a significant character are taking place in the definition of work. More and more people will be working from home, participating in gig economies, and adopting flexible job arrangements. This transformation necessitates a reevaluation of policies pertaining to the labor market, social safety nets, and educational systems in order to accommodate the requirements of a dynamic workforce that is always evolving. Initiatives aimed at upskilling and reskilling individuals will be essential in order to guarantee employability in a labor market that is undergoing fast change.

The Prospects for Technology:

Automation and machines with artificial intelligence:

There will be further developments in artificial intelligence (AI) and automation, which will result in the transformation of industries and job roles.

Despite the fact that automation may result in the loss of jobs in certain industries, it also creates opportunities for new positions that require a high level of expertise.

Requiring regulatory frameworks and responsible development procedures will be necessary in order to address the ethical aspects of artificial intelligence, which include concerns over algorithmic prejudice and privacy.

As well as Connectivity:

The broad implementation of 5G technology will bring about a revolution in connection and make it possible to implement the Internet of Things (IoT) on a scale that has never been seen before. The characteristics of 5G, which include high speeds and low latency, will make significant contributions to the development of breakthroughs in fields such as augmented reality, smart cities, and driverless vehicles. It is important to note that the spread of 5G networks would necessitate substantial expenditures in infrastructure as well as considerations regarding cybersecurity.

Innovations in Biotechnology and Regarding Healthcare:

The landscape of medicine and the delivery of healthcare will be subject to a transformation as a result of developments in biotechnology, genetics, and healthcare technology. The results of healthcare are about to undergo a sea change as a result of the advent of personalized medicine, gene therapies, and novel diagnostics. The use of technology into healthcare, such as telemedicine and health monitoring devices, will contribute to the development of healthcare systems that are more easily accessible and more effective.

The Technologies of the Environment:

The critical nature of combating climate change will be the impetus for technological advancements in the environmental sector. The use of sustainable behaviors, energy storage systems, and renewable energy sources will be at the forefront of efforts to reduce the negative effects of climate change. The rise of circular economies, which involve the reuse and recycling of resources, will become more prevalent as civilizations search for alternatives that are less harmful to the environment.

The Challenges Facing Cybersecurity:

The growing reliance on digital technologies leads to the emergence of issues in the realm of cybersecurity. The risk of cyber threats and attacks is increasing as the number of people connected to the internet increases and the value of data increases. It will be necessary for governments, organizations, and individuals to make investments in effective cybersecurity measures, legislation, and international coordination in order to protect digital assets and privacy.

Exploration of Space and Commercialization of Satellites:

The exploration of space and the commercialization of space are both primed to experience substantial advancements in the near future. Private businesses are actively participating in the exploration of space, the deployment of satellites, and even the development of plans for space tourism. As a result of this tendency, new prospects for economic growth, technical improvements, and international partnerships in space-related endeavors are opening up.

Considerations of an Ethical Nature in Technology:

Ethical considerations that are associated with the utilization of technology will play an increasingly prominent role. Regulatory frameworks will be shaped by conversations about the protection of personal data, the transparency of algorithmic processes, and the responsible application of developing technology. Facial recognition, biometrics, and artificial intelligence are examples of technologies that will demand rigorous examination and public discussion due to the ethical implications they may have.

Perspectives on Society:

Changes in the Population:

There will be significant repercussions for societies all around the world as a result of demographic trends, which include decreasing birth rates and increasing elderly populations. The demand for healthcare services, eldercare, and pension systems is expected to expand, which will require modifications to be made to public policies and the structures that provide social assistance.

Cities that are smart and urbanization:

There will be a continuation of urbanization trends, which will result in the expansion of megacities and the creation of sophisticated cities. Efficiency, sustainability, and the overall quality of life will all be improved as a result of the use of technology into urban design, transportation, and resource management. Nevertheless, careful attention will be required in order to address the difficulties that are associated with infrastructure, cost, and equal access to resources.

Health Preparedness on a Global Scale:

The reality of the COVID-19 pandemic has brought to light the significance of being prepared for the health of people all around the world. In order to effectively respond to future health crises, it is anticipated that societies will make investments in the improvement of healthcare infrastructure, early warning systems, and international cooperation. In the future, public health initiatives will heavily emphasize the importance of being prepared for pandemics.

Movements pursuing social justice:

Social justice movements that are still active and advocate for equality, diversity, and inclusion will continue to have an impact on the norms that society adheres to. It is inevitable that legislation, corporate practices, and public discourse will be influenced by the demand for social and racial justice, gender equality, and rights for LGBTQ+ individuals. This will continue to be the case as technology continues to play a role in amplifying these voices and supporting social movements.

Evolution of the Educational System:

Traditional educational practices are undergoing a revolution that is being pushed by the proliferation of digital technology and the shifting dynamics of the workforce. It is expected that personalized education models, online learning, and virtual classrooms will develop into more widespread practices. Initiatives for lifelong learning and programs for upskilling will be necessary in order to guarantee that individuals will continue to be adaptable in a labor market that is always changing.

Awareness of Mental Health Issues:

Because of the growing awareness of mental health issues and the significance of well-being, societies will be more likely to prioritize the provision of mental health support. The elimination of stigma associated with mental health issues, the enhancement of access to mental health treatments, and the creation of supportive settings in the workplace will all play an important role in the promotion of general societal well-being.

Local identity with the process of cultural globalization:

Shared global narratives will continue to be shaped by cultural globalization, which will be made possible by the proliferation of digital connectedness. There will, however, be a concurrent focus placed on the preservation and celebration of local identities as well as the diversity of cultural traditions. The cohabitation of local expressions and global influences will lead to the creation of a rich tapestry of cultural contacts to be woven together.

The outlook for the future is a canvas that is painted with a wide variety of opportunities, challenges, and possibilities simultaneously. Economic recovery, technical improvements, and social shifts are all intertwined threads that collectively create the trajectory of human progress. Human progress is shaped by these threads. Adaptive policies, ethical concerns, and a dedication to inclusivity and sustainability are all necessary components for successfully navigating this complicated landscape.

When it comes to guiding societies toward a future that is marked by resilience, innovation, and shared prosperity, the responsibilities that governments, businesses, and individuals play are of primary importance. Humanity has the potential to harness the power of change and construct a future that represents our common ambitions for a better society if it is willing to embrace the challenges of the future with foresight and collaborate with one another.

8.1 Projections for the trajectory of the U.S. economy

The trajectory of the economy of the United States is a subject of continual analysis and conjecture. This trajectory is influenced by a wide variety of elements, which include economic policies, global dynamics, technology breakthroughs, and societal shifts. When we look into the future, we make a number of important projections that shape the route that the economy of the United States is expected to take. The purpose of this analysis is to investigate these projections by taking into account a variety of factors, including economic recovery following the epidemic, technological improvements, legislative decisions, and global impacts, all of which will together define the path that the United States economy will take in the years to come.

The Economic Recovery Following the Pandemic:

Employment and the Growth of the GDP:

A permanent imprint has been made on the economy of the United States as a result of the aftermath of the COVID-19 pandemic. GDP growth and employment rates are the two most important factors that will determine the trajectory of the economic recovery. The impact of the epidemic is projected to lessen, and analysts foresee a resurgence in economic activity. More specifically, they anticipate that GDP growth will resume momentum. Within the context of this recovery, the restoration of jobs that were lost as a result of the pandemic is an essential component, with the primary goals being the reduction of unemployment rates and the promotion of labor participation.

Policies Relating to Finance and Money:

The success of monetary and fiscal policy will be a critical factor in determining the nature of the recovery that will occur after the pandemic. The control of interest rates by the Federal Reserve, the adoption of quantitative easing measures, and the execution of specific fiscal stimuli by the government will all have an impact on consumer spending, investment, and the overall sentiment of the economy. It will be a challenging endeavor for policymakers to find a balanced approach that allows them to promote the recovery while also limiting inflationary pressures.

Dynamic Forces in Sectors:

The way in which particular industries operate will have an impact on the path that the economy of the United States will take.

There is a possibility that the recovery of businesses such as travel, hospitality, and traditional retail will take longer time than anticipated. However, it is anticipated that industries such as technology, healthcare, and renewable energy would contribute considerably to growth. The strength of the economy as a whole will be determined by the degree to which businesses are able to adjust to shifting patterns of consumer behavior and the dynamics of the market.

The development of new technologies:

The Transformation of Digital:

The United States economy is on the cusp of undergoing a continuous digital transformation, which will have an impact on the trajectory of a variety of industries. Business models and labor procedures are going to undergo significant transformations as a result of technological advancements such as artificial intelligence, automation, and the Internet of Things. The implementation of this change has the potential to result in increased productivity, improved competitiveness, and the creation of new economic opportunities.

Innovation Centers and Financial Investments in Research:

As part of the forecast for the economy of the United States, it is anticipated that innovation hubs will continue to grow and that investments in research and development will expand. Cities and regions that encourage collaboration between businesses, research institutions, and startups are more likely to be the driving force behind technological advancements. Support from the government for research efforts, particularly in fields such as information technology, clean energy, and biotechnology, will contribute to the continuation of innovation.

As well as Connectivity:

There are many different industries that are expected to undergo significant changes as a result of the broad implementation of 5G technology. With 5G networks, the development and implementation of applications in areas such as smart cities, driverless vehicles, and augmented reality will be accelerated. This is because 5G networks offer better connection and lower latency. It is anticipated that this technological breakthrough would contribute to the expansion of the economy and the creation of new commercial prospects.

Policy Landscape:

An Investment in the Infrastructure:

Policy decisions made by the government, such as those on projected investments in infrastructure, will have an impact on the trajectory of the economy in the United States.

To boost economic activity, generate jobs, and strengthen the nation's long-term competitiveness, the execution of large-scale infrastructure projects, such as improvements to transportation networks, expansion of broadband, and programs to promote renewable energy, has the potential to be implemented.

The Policies of Trade and International Relations:

The course of the United States economy is inextricably connected to the nation's policies regarding trade and international relations. Alterations in trade agreements, geopolitical dynamics, and diplomatic ties have the potential to have an effect on international supply chains and distribution networks. It will be a challenging endeavor for policymakers to find a middle ground between the protection of domestic industry and the promotion of economic cooperation for the global community.

Policies Regarding the Environment and ESG:

It is expected that economic policies will be influenced by the increasing emphasis placed on environmental, social, and governance (ESG) factors. The United States of America is anticipated to experience a heightened emphasis on sustainability, which will be accompanied by legislation that promotes programs to reduce carbon emissions, renewable energy, and sustainable corporate practices. The economic landscape will be impacted by the incorporation of environmental, social, and governance (ESG) elements into investment decisions and company plans.

Considerations Regarding Social and Demographic Factors:

Changes in the Population:

There will be a significant impact on the trajectory of the United States economy brought about by demographic changes such as aging populations and shifting dynamics within the workforce. Both the labor force participation and pension systems are expected to face challenges as a result of the aging workforce and the population of retirees. In order to maintain economic growth, it will be necessary to modify policy in order to reflect changes in the overall population.

Dynamics of the Labor Market:

The very nature of employment is changing, which has repercussions for the economy of the United States. Work that is performed from a remote location, gig economies, and flexible employment models are becoming increasingly common. The projections indicate that there will be a sustained move toward remote and hybrid work arrangements, which will have an effect on urbanization patterns, real estate markets, and the demand for specific types of talents.

Instruction and the Development of the Workforce:

When it comes to determining the future course of the United States economy, investments in education and workforce development are absolutely necessary. The ability of the workforce to adjust to new technology developments and shifting industrial demands will be contingent on the availability of education and training programs that are pertinent to the specific needs of employees. It is anticipated that efforts aimed at lifelong learning and cooperation between educational institutions and companies would become increasingly prominent.

Challenges and Uncertainties in Regard to:

There are pressures of inflation:

Inflation is a serious worry that is associated with the trajectory of the United States economy, which is not without its obstacles. There have been worries voiced over the possibility of inflationary pressures as a result of the significant fiscal and monetary measures that have been implemented in response to the outbreak. It will be a challenging endeavor for policymakers to find a middle ground between fostering economic recovery and controlling inflation.

Economic Dynamics on a Global Scale:

It is impossible to predict what will happen in the global economy because of its linked nature. There are a number of factors that have the potential to have a spill-over effect on the economy of the United States, including international trade issues, geopolitical crises, and global economic slowdowns. In order to maintain economic growth throughout time, it will be essential to possess the ability to navigate and adjust well to shifting global dynamics.

Planned measures for health:

The path that the economy of the United States will take is inextricably linked to concerns regarding health. The resilience of the healthcare system and, by extension, the economy as a whole will be impacted by the continued handling of public health crises, the readiness to deal with the possibility of pandemics in the future, and the equitable allocation of healthcare resources.

There is a complex interaction between economic, technological, policy, and social issues, and the estimates for the evolution of the economy in the United States reflect this interaction. In order for the nation to successfully navigate the post-pandemic landscape, it will be essential for them to demonstrate resilience, adaptability, and smart decision-making. A positive trajectory for the economy of the United States will be contributed to by proactive policies that encourage economic recovery, technological innovation, social inclusion, and sustainability. As the nation plots its way into the future, the potential for growth, innovation, and societal progress continues to be substantial, despite the fact that difficulties and uncertainties continue to exist.

8.2 Key factors that could influence economic recovery

As nations work to recover from the economic effects of the COVID-19 pandemic and other global difficulties, it is becoming increasingly important to have a solid understanding of the key components that determine economic recovery. A complex interplay of variables, ranging from governmental decisions and technology developments to global dynamics and cultural upheavals, is responsible for shaping the trajectory of recovery. These variables include these and more. Within the scope of this analysis, the most important elements that are anticipated to have an impact on economic development and recovery in the years to come are investigated.

Stimuli for the Fiscal System and Policy Measures:

Policies of the Monetary System and Interest Rates:

Monetary policies are one of the most important roles that central banks play in the process of economic recovery. There is a correlation between the management of interest rates and the price of borrowing money, decisions about investments, and general economic activity. The economy receives a boost from a monetary policy that is accommodative and has low interest rates. This policy stimulates borrowing and spending, effectively stimulating the economy.

Stimuli to the economy and spending by the government:

Fiscal policies implemented by the government, such as stimulus packages and public expenditure, are powerful instruments that can be utilized to kickstart the economic recovery process. In addition to contributing to total economic growth, investments in social programs, healthcare, and infrastructure all contribute to the creation of jobs and the stimulation of demand. It is absolutely necessary to implement budgetary measures in a timely manner and with a specific purpose in order to mitigate the effects of economic downturns.

Managing the Inflation Cycle:

It is essential for policymakers to take into mind the importance of striking a balance between fostering economic recovery and controlling inflation. If demand is higher than supply, there is a possibility that inflation will occur, despite the fact that stimulus measures infuse liquidity into the economy. By implementing measures that handle inflationary pressures without limiting economic progress, central banks are required to fulfill their responsibility.

Innovations and technological advancements:

The Transformation of Digital:

Technological innovations, particularly those linked with digital transformation, play a crucial influence in determining the course of economic recovery.

To better react to shifting market dynamics, increase efficiency, and propel innovation, industries that embrace digital technology, automation, and artificial intelligence are in a better position to do so. There is a correlation between the use of technology into company models and increased strength and resilience.

Financial Investments in Research and Development (R&D):

The path that the economic recovery will take is impacted by the investments that are made in new research and development. In order to foster innovation and the creation of new technologies, governments, industries, and academic institutions that place a priority on research and development (R&D) participate. Research and development advances in fields such as healthcare, renewable energy, and information technology have the potential to propel economic expansion and give rise to the establishment of new industries.

Infrastructure for digital media:

In this day and age, the availability of a robust digital infrastructure is a necessary condition for economic recovery. An environment that is conducive to technological innovation can be created by investments in areas such as the extension of broadband networks, the development of 5G networks, and cybersecurity. For the purpose of supporting remote work, e-commerce, and the entire digitalization of economic activity, a digital infrastructure that is both accessible and dependable is essential.

The Dynamics of the Global Economy:

Regulatory Frameworks for International Trade and Cooperation:

The dynamics of the global economy, which include trade policies and international collaboration, have a substantial impact on the economic recovery. Trade ties that are open and collaborative can be beneficial to nations because they allow for the diversification of markets and the sharing of resources. Policies pertaining to trade that make it easier for commodities and services to travel around the world contribute to the growth and stability of the global economy.

Continuity of geopolitical order:

Stability in geopolitical affairs is an essential component that plays a role in economic recovery. These factors, along with geopolitical wars, trade tensions, and political uncertainties, have the potential to cause volatility in the financial markets and to disrupt global supply networks. In order to contribute to a more stable economic environment on a global scale, nations' efforts to cultivate diplomatic relations and engage in multilateral cooperation are essential.

Considerations Regarding the World's Health:

There is a direct correlation between the worldwide response to health emergencies, such as pandemics, and the economic recovery that occurs. The ability of nations to withstand the effects of health-related shocks is improved by international collaboration in areas such as the distribution of vaccines, the support of healthcare infrastructure, and the preparation for emergencies. Having the capacity to manage difficulties pertaining to global health leads to an economic climate that is more predictable.

Aspects Relating to Society and the Population:

Dynamics of the Labor Market:

It is essential to the economic recovery that the dynamics of the labor market be present. There are a number of factors that determine the rate of recovery, including unemployment rates, workforce participation, and the ability of workers to adjust to changing industries. A workforce that is more resilient can be fostered by governments and corporations that invest in workforce development, initiatives to upskill workers, and policies that allow for greater flexibility in the labor market.

The Confidence of Consumers and Their Spending:

A significant factor in the economic recovery is the confidence of consumers. Demand and overall economic growth are both influenced by the propensity of consumers to engage in economic activities such as spending, investing, and other forms of economic activity. Instilling confidence, protecting consumer rights, and ensuring financial stability are all policies that contribute to a successful economic recovery.

Changes in the Population:

There are a number of demographic aspects that have an impact on economic recovery. These elements include population growth, aging populations, and labor makeup. Countries that have favorable demographic profiles, such as a young and expanding workforce, have the potential to experience greater economic dynamism and productivity. Making adjustments to policy in order to handle demographic issues, such as an aging population, is absolutely necessary in order to achieve sustained recovery.

Considerations Regarding the Environment and Long-Term Sustainability:

Policies that are Ethical and Sustainable:

Considerations pertaining to the environment and sustainability are becoming increasingly intertwined with economic recovery.

When governments and businesses implement policies that are environmentally friendly and sustainable, they contribute to an economy that is more robust and focused on the future. The alignment of economic growth and environmental conservation can be achieved by investments in renewable energy, sustainable infrastructure, and circular economies.

Resistance to the Climate:

It is necessary to implement policies that are climate-resilient since the effects of climate change provide obstacles to the economic recovery process. Long-term economic stability can be achieved by investments in infrastructure that take into account climatic risks, sustainable land use practices, and regulations that address environmental degradation.

Obstacles and Things to Take Into Account:

Getting Ready for a Pandemics:

One of the most important factors that will determine the success of the economic recovery is the capacity to handle and respond to health issues. For the purpose of minimizing the economic effects of future health emergencies, investments in hospital infrastructure, vaccine delivery networks, and international cooperation in pandemic preparedness are all important factors.

Both the Levels of Debt and the Financial Stability:

When it comes to economic recovery, high amounts of governmental and private debt can be seen as a potential obstacle. Both firms and governments have a responsibility to strike a balance between the concern for long-term financial stability and the requirement for fiscal stimulus. In order to support a prolonged recovery, it is necessary to have prudent financial management, debt restructuring, and transparent reporting of financial information.

Growth That Is Inclusive:

It is imperative that inclusive growth be prioritized throughout economic recovery in order to address social inequities. The implementation of policies that prioritize the reduction of income disparity, the promotion of social mobility, and the guarantee of equal access to opportunities contributes to the development of a society that is strong and socially cohesive.

The path that the economic recovery will take would be determined by the dynamic interaction of a number of different elements. In order to successfully negotiate the difficulties of post-pandemic recovery, technological transformations, and global issues, policymakers, corporations, and societies must work together successfully.

For the purpose of constructing a resilient and sustainable economic future, it is vital to take a comprehensive approach that incorporates both fiscal and monetary policies, embraces technology breakthroughs, encourages international cooperation, and places a priority on social and environmental issues. In the process of nations charting their road toward recovery, strategic decision-making that is aligned with these important elements will play a major role in deciding the success of efforts to revitalize the economy.

Chapter 9

Conclusion

It is necessary to have a detailed grasp of the underlying causes, manifestations, and potential pathways towards recovery in order to comprehend the phenomena of a nation's economic decline, which is extremely complicated and multifaceted. Because of its position as a worldwide economic powerhouse, the United States of America has been able to endure a number of economic downturns throughout its history. In this extensive conclusion, we delve into the important lessons that were drawn from our investigation of the economic fall in the United States. We discuss the intricate interaction of forces, the ramifications that were felt across a variety of industries, and the prospective possibilities for recovery.

Insights from an Overview of the Economic Downturn Analysis:

In the context of history:

It is vital to have a solid understanding of the historical backdrop of economic downturns in the United States in order to have a complete comprehension of the dynamic nature of economic issues. The Great Depression of the 1930s and the more recent recessions that have been precipitated by financial crises and global events are examples of historical patterns that provide significant insights on the resilience and potential for recovery of the nation.

Relationships between economies around the world:

In the current state of the global economy, the connectivity of nations is brought into sharper focus. There is no such thing as an isolated economic collapse in the United States; rather, it is frequently linked with global issues such as trade relations, geopolitical dynamics, and the impact of worldwide events. Understanding the complex web of factors that have an effect on the economy of the United States is improved by conducting an analysis of the global context.

Technological Changes and Developments:

Both the high speed of technical improvements and the arrival of the Fourth Industrial Revolution have significant repercussions for the economic downturn and the subsequent recovery. Despite the fact that technology has the potential to be a driver of innovation and prosperity, it also presents a number of issues, including the displacement of jobs, disruptions to industries, and the digital divide. It is essential to successfully navigate these shifts in order to construct the path that the economic recovery will take.

The Implications for Policy:

It is impossible to exaggerate the significance of the role that government policies play in responding to economic collapse. When it comes to minimizing the effects of economic downturns, critical factors include the implementation of fiscal and monetary policies, the establishment of regulatory frameworks, and the capacity to quickly adjust to shifting conditions. When it comes to formulating successful methods to deal with economic difficulties, it is helpful to examine previous policy responses because it provides significant lessons.

Industry-Specific Obstacles and Challenges:

Dynamics of the Labor Market:

The labor market is an important indicator of the state of the economy, and the oscillations that occur in it during times of economic depression have far-reaching repercussions. The most important problems include the increasing rates of unemployment, the changes in employment patterns, and the difficulties associated with re-skilling the workforce. Policymakers have a responsibility to handle these phenomena in order to guarantee that the labor market will continue to be flexible and responsive to developing economic trends.

The resilience of the financial sector:

During times of crisis, the financial sector, which is frequently at the center of economic downturns, is subjected to stress. The broader financial infrastructure, as well as regulatory authorities and banking institutions, all play important roles in the establishment and maintenance of stability. The critical role that good financial management, regulatory vigilance, and proactive measures play in preventing systemic risks is highlighted by the lessons that can be learned from previous recessions.

Particular Obstacles Facing the Industry:

During periods of economic decline, several industries face a variety of distinct obstacles. Particularly vulnerable to the effects of market changes are industries such as retail, hospitality, and manufacturing. When it comes to determining their resilience and ability to recover, the ability of industries to successfully adapt, innovate, and diversify is of critical importance. The analysis of these difficulties that are specific to the industry provides information that can be used to build recovery strategies that are tailored.

The Influence on Society and Culture:

Social Disparities and the Unequal Distribution of Income:

Whenever there is a collapse in the economy, it frequently exacerbates the social gaps that already exist, which results in increased economic inequality and differences in access to opportunities. It is not just an issue of social fairness but also of critical importance for the development of an economy that is more inclusive and resilient to change that these inequities be addressed. In the long run, the effects of economic downturns on society can be mitigated by the implementation of policies that prioritize inclusive growth and social mobility.

Alterations and alterations to cultural norms:

It is possible for a fall in economic conditions to spark cultural transformations and adjustments within a civilization. Examples of cultural responses to economic issues include shifts in consumer behavior, attitudes toward employment, and an increased emphasis on ethical and environmentally responsible company practices with regard to sustainability. It is beneficial for communities, businesses, and politicians to get an understanding of these cultural processes since it delivers useful insights.

The Implications for Politics and Public Policy:

Various Interventions and Policies of the Government:

It is important to the role that the government plays in determining the path that the economic recovery will take. Policies that include regulatory frameworks, monetary interventions, and fiscal stimulus packages are all powerful tools that policymakers have at their disposal. On the other hand, the efficacy of these policies is contingent upon their timeliness, their congruence with the reality of the economy, and their capacity to strike a balance between providing relief in the short term and ensuring their sustainable operation in the long run.

Analysis of Political Decision-Making and Its Effects on the Economy:

It is important to note that the decisions that political leaders make during periods of economic collapse have long-lasting implications. The ability to execute substantial reforms, political will, and cooperation amongst members of both parties are all extremely important. In order to have a better understanding of the durability of democratic institutions in the face of economic crises, it is necessary to provide an evaluation of the political environment and the decisions made by leaders.

Consequences on Society:

Effects on the Distribution of Income:

The deterioration of the economy frequently makes income inequality worse, which in turn causes a domino effect across society. A widening wealth gap is caused by a number of factors, including unequal access to education and healthcare, unequal distribution of economic opportunities, and inequities in wealth concentration. The implementation of comprehensive policies that place an emphasis on inclusive economic growth is necessary in order to address it.

Social and Cultural Consequences This includes:

During times of economic downturn, the social and cultural architecture of a society goes through a process of metamorphosis. There are clear indications of shifts in lifestyle, values, and the dynamics of the community. For the purpose of predicting the requirements of society, promoting resilience, and maintaining social cohesiveness during difficult times, it is vital to have a solid understanding of these implications.

Obstacles that are Unique to the Industry:

An Examination of the Industries That Are Being Hit Hard by the Economic Downturn:

When there is a downturn in the economy, different industries experience varied degrees of an influence. The majority of the negative effects of decreased consumer spending are typically felt in industries such as travel, hospitality, and traditional retail. By gaining an understanding of the difficulties that are particular to each industry, focused interventions and recovery plans can be developed to meet the specific requirements of the industries that have been impacted.

Considerations in Regard to the Development of New Technologies and Innovations:

Innovation and technical progress can be stifled or accelerated by economic collapse, depending on the circumstances. The demand for efficiency and cost-effectiveness may be the driving force behind the adoption of new technologies, despite the fact that budgetary constraints may limit investments in research and development. One can gain a more detailed understanding of the resilience and adaptation of specific industries by doing an analysis of the consequences for innovation in those industries.

Concerning the Possible Solutions:

Recommendations for Public Policy Intended to Revitalize the Economy:

An approach that takes into account multiple aspects is required in order to formulate successful policy suggestions for economic regeneration. Specifically targeted budgetary initiatives, regulatory reforms, and strategic investments in fundamental industries are all included in this. For the purpose of promoting a healthy and resilient economic recovery, it is vital to put into effect policies that value sustainability, inclusion, and innovation.

The Function of Public-Private Partnerships in the Process of Recovering:

There is a growing recognition that public-private partnerships (PPPs) are an essential component of the recovery toolkit. Accelerating infrastructure projects, stimulating job creation, and leveraging various resources are all possible outcomes that can be achieved through the coordinated efforts of government and commercial enterprises. Having transparent procurement processes, risk-sharing systems, and clear communication between stakeholders are all essential to the success of public-private partnerships (PPPs).

Prospects for the Future:

Tendencies and Obstacles That Are Anticipated:

It is necessary to have a clear awareness of projected trends and problems in order to successfully navigate the future. In the future, the trajectory of the United States economy will be influenced by factors such as the post-pandemic recovery, technology breakthroughs, altering labor market dynamics, and global economic shifts. Governments, organizations, and society all need to maintain their capacity for adaptation and proactivity in order to effectively meet new issues.

Future prospects in terms of society, technology, and the economy:

There is a close relationship between the perspective of the United States in terms of its economy, technology, and society. Technological improvements and economic tactics are both influenced by societal trends, which include demographic shifts and cultural adjustments. It is essential to have a comprehensive strategy that takes into account the development of society as a whole in order to achieve economic growth that is both sustainable and inclusive.

An investigation of the circumstances that led to the fall of the economy in the United States reveals a complex web of interrelated elements, difficulties, and possible remedies.

A holistic and collaborative approach to recovery is required because of the complex web of forces that have been exerted on the economy of the United States, which includes both historical perspectives and modern analysis.

The resiliency that has been shown in the face of previous economic downturns serves as a beacon of hope for the United States of America, which is currently struggling with economic issues. To set the path for a healthy recovery, it is possible to implement legislative measures that are effective, interventions that are targeted, and a commitment to providing inclusivity and sustainability.

It is vital that stakeholders acknowledge the dynamic nature of the global economy, the transformative potential of technology, and the necessity of addressing societal imbalances in order to chart the route forward. By encouraging innovation, welcoming change, and placing a priority on the well-being of communities, the United States of America has the potential to emerge from economic collapse with a revitalized sense of power and adaptability thanks to these strategies.

The result of the investigation into the deterioration of the economy in the United States serves as a call to action. It is a call for collaborative efforts, informed decision-making, and a shared commitment to the construction of an economic future that is robust and sustainable. Both the difficulties and the potential for constructive change, growth, and advancement are tremendous. However, the challenges are also substantial.

9.1 Recapitulation of major findings

In light of the fact that we are coming to the end of our in-depth investigation of the economic downfall of the United States, it is vital that we summarize the most important facts that have arisen from the extensive examination. Due to the complex nature of economic decline, it is necessary to have a detailed grasp of the historical circumstances, global interconnectedness, sector-specific issues, societal implications, and the role that policies and interventions play. In order to establish the groundwork for well-informed policies and solutions, the purpose of this recapitulation is to bring together the most important findings that shed light on the complexities of the economic slide.

Historical Context: Understanding Patterns of Resilience in the World

When conducting an analysis of the reduction in economic activity, it is essential to take into account the historical backdrop, as one of the foundational results. There have been numerous economic downturns that the United States of America has endured throughout its history. These include the Great Depression, recessions that were brought on by financial crises, and the most recent challenges that have been brought about by the global COVID-19 pandemic.

In order to successfully navigate the complexities of the current economic landscape, it is helpful to have a solid understanding of the historical patterns of recovery, resilience, and adaptability.

The Interconnectedness of the World's Economy: The Intertwined Threads of Influence

A key discovery is the indisputable impact that the interconnectivity of economies across the world has had on the path that the economy of the United States has taken. The fall of the economy is rarely a singular occurrence; rather, it is closely connected to a variety of global elements, including trade relations, geopolitical dynamics, and international events. When the interconnected strands of influence are taken into account, it becomes clear that there is a pressing requirement for a holistic approach to economic analysis and recovery measures that take into account the larger global context.

Catalysts and Challenges in the Context of Technological Transformations

One of the most important aspects to consider when attempting to comprehend the downfall of the economy is the quick pace of technical improvements. Technology, while acting as a stimulus for innovation, efficiency, and prosperity, simultaneously offers issues such as the displacement of jobs, disruptions to industries, and the digital divide. Some of these challenges are listed below. The trajectory of recovery is shaped in large part by technological transformations, which need the development of adaptive strategies that capitalize on the positive features of innovation while simultaneously reducing its negative implications.

Concerning the Implications of Policy: The Crucial Function of the Government

There is a significant discovery that pertains to the essential role that government policies play in the process of responding to economic collapse. There have been a number of factors that have emerged as crucial, including the efficiency of monetary and fiscal policies, regulatory frameworks, and the capacity to effectively respond to shifting conditions. Utilizing strategic interventions that are tailored to solve the specific issues that are brought about by economic downturns, policymakers are required to strike a careful balance between providing relief in the short term and ensuring long-term sustainability.

Challenges that are specific to the sector: navigating the dynamics of the industry

During the period of economic collapse, the analysis shed light on the various obstacles that were encountered by various industries. The dynamics of the labor market, the resiliency of the financial sector, and the issues that are peculiar to the business all highlight the necessity of targeted solutions. Reduced consumer spending frequently has a disproportionately negative impact on some industries, including travel, hospitality, and traditional retail. This highlights the significance of developing flexible strategies and recovery plans that are specifically customized to each industry.

The Influence on Society and Culture: Understanding the Workings of Societal Development

There are significant ramifications that a fall in the economy has on society and culture, which contribute to changes in lifestyle, values, and the dynamics of the community. Inequality in terms of income, social inequities, and cultural adaptations are all interrelated factors that require attention. It is necessary to implement comprehensive policies that prioritize inclusive economic growth, social mobility, and cultural resilience in order to address the socioeconomic implications that have been caused.

Regarding the Nexus of Decision-Making, the Political and Policy Implications of the Situation

Among the most important discoveries is the connection between political decision-making and the outcomes of economic activity. It is the policies and interventions of the government that have a key influence in deciding the path that recovery will take. These policies and interventions are defined by political will, bipartisan cooperation, and the ability to enforce effective reforms. The political climate and the choices that were taken by leaders during times of economic downturn are two of the most important factors to take into consideration while attempting to comprehend the durability of democratic institutions.

Societal Consequences: The Ongoing Impact on Communities and Communities in Question

In addition to having an effect on economic indicators, the societal ramifications of a declining economy have a dramatic influence on the communities that are affected. The need for policies that prioritize the well-being of communities is highlighted by the fact that income disparity, social and cultural implications, and the challenges faces by particular demographic groups all highlight the importance of such policies. The development of resilience within communities is absolutely necessary in order to facilitate a sustainable recovery.

Challenges that are specific to different industries: individualized strategies for resilience

The examination of industries that are bearing the brunt of the economic downturn indicated the necessity of individualized ways to meet the difficulties that are specific to the industry. When it comes to developing tailored recovery strategies, having an awareness of the subtleties of each sector is essential. This includes understanding the implications on established businesses as well as the disruptions that are driven by technology. In order to ensure the resilience of a variety of industries, it is essential to have regulations that are flexible and innovative, as well as technical breakthroughs and innovations.

The development of a recovery road map is one of the potential solutions.

Given the relevance of strategic policymaking for economic regeneration, the investigation into alternative solutions brought to light the importance of this process.

A comprehensive road map for recovery was found to include recommendations for targeted budgetary measures, regulatory reforms, and the role of public-private partnerships. These recommendations emerged as important components. Giving sustainability, diversity, and innovation a high priority will be absolutely necessary in order to construct an economic future that is both resilient and adaptable.

The Prospects for the Future: Identifying Emerging Trends and Obstacles

An important factor that emerged as a forward-looking consideration was the anticipation of future trends and obstacles. The path that the United States economy will take will be determined by factors such as the post-pandemic recovery, technology improvements, the dynamics of the labor market, and global economic shifts. In order to achieve economic growth that is both sustainable and inclusive, it is essential to take a proactive and adaptable approach that takes into account the overall development of society.

Following the summary of the most important findings, a comprehensive overview of the complex web of causes that are contributing to the economic deterioration in the United States is provided. Each study contributes to a holistic perspective that informs recovery measures. This perspective encompasses everything from the impact of technology transformations to the historical resilience of the population. The insights that were gathered from this comprehensive research serve as a compass for informed decision-making, adaptive policies, and a resilient route toward a sustainable economic future. This is especially important as the nation navigates the challenges that come with an economic downturn.

9.2 Call to action for stakeholders in addressing economic decline

During this time when the United States is struggling to overcome the challenges of economic decline, it is vital that stakeholders from a wide range of sectors respond with a collective and unequivocal call to action. Because of the complex web of causes that contribute to economic downturns, it is necessary for individuals, corporations, civil society organizations, and government agencies to work together in a coordinated and cooperative strategy. Within the scope of this in-depth examination, we investigate the fundamental elements that constitute a call to action, putting particular emphasis on the necessity of strategic collaboration, innovative solutions, and a dedication to inclusion and sustainability.

The Leadership of the Government: Formulating Policies That Are Both Informed and Adaptable

Active Measures Regarding the Budget:

The development and execution of fiscal policies that are guided by relevant information is a crucial part of the role that government entities play in addressing the decline of the economy.

A call to action necessitates the implementation of proactive measures, such as tailored stimulus packages, investments in infrastructure, and tax incentives, in order to revitalize economic activity and generate employment opportunities.

A Harmonization of Monetary Policy:

It is absolutely necessary for the government and central banks to work together in order to successfully align monetary policy with the ever-changing global economic environment. It is possible to contribute to the maintenance of a stable economic environment by ensuring that the rates of interest, inflation targets, and quantitative easing measures are all synced with the requirements of the recovery.

Changes to the Regulations:

When it comes to promoting innovation, providing assistance to enterprises, and reducing systemic risks, a regulatory framework that is responsive is absolutely necessary." It is vital that stakeholders push for regulations that are streamlined in order to strike a balance between the critical requirement for economic dynamism and the imperative of preserving public interests.

Innovativeness, adaptability, and social responsibility are the three pillars of business resilience

Innovative Technological Practices:

As a means of improving their efficiency, competitiveness, and resilience, businesses have little choice but to embrace technological innovation. As part of a call to action, it is necessary to cultivate an environment that encourages innovation, to make investments in research and development, and to make use of technologies that can propel growth while simultaneously solving societal concerns.

Strategies that are Adaptic:

The capacity of organizations to adjust to the ever-changing dynamics of the market is of the utmost importance. Businesses will be in a better position to weather economic storms and contribute to overall recovery efforts if they take a proactive approach to strategic planning, diversification, and the implementation of sustainable practices.

Responsibility Towards Society:

A commitment to social responsibility is an essential component of a call to action, as businesses play an essential role in the overall well-being of society.

Businesses should promote ethical practices, community engagement, and programs that address social and environmental concerns in addition to commercial considerations. Additionally, businesses should value the environment.

Engagement of Civil Society: Promoting Inclusivity and Advocacy for Change Initiatives That Are Inclusive:

In order to promote inclusiveness and advocate for the well-being of populations who are marginalized, organizations that are part of civil society play an extremely important role. The act of supporting and engaging in activities that promote equality, social justice, and access to opportunities for all members of society is an example of a call to action because it entails taking action.

Outreach in the Field of Education:

Participation in educational outreach activities is one way in which civil society can make a contribution to the development of society. Education is a potent tool for societal development. The empowerment of individuals to manage economic uncertainty can be achieved through the promotion of digital literacy, the facilitation of workforce training programs, and the enhancement of access to quality education systems.

Support for Social Policies and Programs:

It is possible for organizations that are part of civil society to be effective advocates for social policies that address issues such as income inequality, inequities in healthcare, and other structural concerns. Participating actively in policy discourse, working together with policymakers, and advocating for projects that put the well-being of society as their top priority are all components of a call to action.

The Empowerment of Individuals: The Construction of Resilient Communities

Understanding of Finances:

Literacy in financial matters is the first step toward individual empowerment. Initiatives that improve financial education and assist individuals in making educated decisions on budgeting, investments, and long-term financial planning are examples of interventions that fall under the category of a call to action.

Entrepreneurship and creative problem solving:

The empowerment of individuals to generate economic possibilities is facilitated by fostering an environment that promotes innovation and entrepreneurship. Through the provision of assistance to small enterprises, startup initiatives, and mentorship programs, it is possible to contribute to the creation of jobs and the development of communities.

Engagement with the Community:

Developing communities that are resilient involves the active participation of both individuals and groups. Community participation, volunteer work, and collaborative initiatives to address local concerns are all forms of action that are included in a call to action. Consolidated communities are the bedrock upon which a more comprehensive economic revival is built.

International Cooperation: Finding Solutions to Global Problems

The Cooperation of Trade:

The importance of international cooperation cannot be overstated in a global economy that is interdependent. The promotion of trade cooperation, the correction of trade imbalances, and the participation in diplomatic initiatives are all examples of calls to action that are intended to promote economic connections that are equitable and mutually beneficial.

Health Initiatives on a Global Scale:

In order to mitigate the continued effects of global health problems, it is necessary for healthcare professionals to work together. In order to improve global health infrastructure, stakeholders should lobby for international efforts that promote health equity, assure access to vaccines and treatments, and ensure that health care is accessible to all.

Good Stewardship of the Environment:

When it comes to achieving a lasting economic recovery, collaborative initiatives to solve environmental concerns are absolutely necessary. In order to contribute to global efforts for a resilient and sustainable future, it is important to participate in international accords, as well as to support projects that promote clean energy and to embrace behaviors that are environmentally responsible.

A rallying cry for collaboration, creativity, and commitment to the well-being of society is the call to action that has been sent to stakeholders in order to counteract the negative effects of economic decline. In the process of overcoming economic issues and contributing to recovery efforts, individuals, businesses, civil society organizations, and government agencies each play distinct roles that are intertwined despite their differences.

A more robust and inclusive economic future can be cooperatively constructed by stakeholders through the formulation of policies that are informed and adaptable, the promotion of corporate resilience, the engagement of civil society, the empowerment of individuals, and participation in international collaboration. Despite the fact that the obstacles are extremely difficult to overcome, there is a significant possibility for good change, creativity, and advancement. Not only do stakeholders contribute to their immediate domains of influence by responding to this call to action, but they also contribute to the overarching objective of promoting a global economy that is both sustainable and prosperous.